Dandelion Resilience

Dandelion Resilience

Finding the Freedom to Bloom

Brandy McCachren

Publishing support provided by
Ignite Press
55 Shaw Ave. Suite 204
Clovis, CA 93612
www.IgnitePress.us

ISBN: 979-8-9911312-0-9
ISBN: 979-8-9911312-1-6 (E-book)

For bulk purchases and for booking, contact:

Brandy McCachren
resilienceroadadvising@gmail.com
www.resilienceroadadvising.com

Because of the dynamic nature of the internet, web addresses or links
contained in this book may have been changed since publication and
may no longer be valid. The content of this book and all expressed opinions
are those of the author and do not reflect the publisher or the publishing team.
The author is solely responsible for all content included herein.

The activities presented in "Seeds of Thought" are curated from various sources
and best practices within the field.
They are intended to provide a compilation of effective strategies
rather than original creations.

Library of Congress Control Number: 2024914559

Cover design by Fouzia Yasin Matin
Edited by Cathy Cruise
Content editing by Lesly Gregory
Interior design by Jetlaunch

FIRST EDITION

This book is dedicated to my unsung hero, Nancy (a.k.a. Nana), who took a leap of faith.
You fought with me and for me, ensuring I had a chance at life.
Your unwavering prayers, boundless love, and steadfast support
have left an indelible mark on my heart.
I am forever grateful and deeply miss you.

"But they who wait for the LORD shall renew their strength;
they shall mount up with wings like eagles;
they shall run and not be weary;
they shall walk and not faint."
Isaiah 40:31

CONTENTS

PART THREE: Rooted Resilience

"So many of us have the vines of past relationships, grievances, and experiences wrapped around us. Maybe around our ankles, tripping us up as we try to move on. Maybe around our waist, letting us stretch and reach for what we want, but never letting us get close enough to grab. Maybe around our neck, choking and suffocating us so we can't even see or think clearly, and preventing us from even realizing there is something beyond the past to reach for."

—Author Unknown

INTRODUCTION

Every one of us carries feelings of our formative years and it shines a light on who we are today. Many carry the weight of traumatic experiences. Some are worse than others. I believe God gives us an ability to forget certain experiences or memories. The ability to forget can provide the capacity to focus on the present and future rather than being weighed down by the past. This concept of self preservation is a defense mechanism the mind employs to cope with overwhelming traumatic events. Letting go of past burdens enables personal growth and clears a path for a fresh start. It's a powerful step forward that allows you to reclaim your future without the weight of your past holding you back. If you find yourself at an impasse, struggling to bridge the gap and make a connection to the depths of your trauma, know you are not alone in your experience. Embracing healing and growth opens up new possibilities for creating a more positive and fulfilling life.

The courage to delve into the depths of my darkest childhood wounds didn't come easily. For decades, I carried a heavy burden of sorrow, hesitating to confront the root of my feelings due to an overwhelming sense of unease. Questions plagued my mind: Why confront the deeply ingrained belief that I was unlovable? Was I strong enough to endure the reemergence of past traumas? Did I possess the emotional intelligence needed to connect with my feelings and transform my pain into a purposeful journey?

These apprehensions weighed heavily on my soul, yet now I recognize that this is my season for healing. The ghosts of my past no longer intimidate me; instead, I face them with newfound strength. I acknowledge that my survival holds profound purpose and value in shaping the person I am today. Though the scars remain, they no longer define me. Instead, they stand as a testament to my immense strength and resilience, narrating a story of survival against all odds.

In these pages, we explore the profound impact of a challenging upbringing on personal growth, while also celebrating the resilience of the human spirit. Drawing inspiration from nature, especially the resilient dandelion, we examine how difficult circumstances may temporarily impede progress. Yet, like dandelions, humans possess adaptability, persistence, and the ability to flourish in diverse conditions. The dandelion symbolizes hope, showcasing our capacity to overcome obstacles and thrive despite adversity. It serves as a reminder of our inherent ability to conquer challenges and prosper, be vibrant and tenacious.

Join me on this healing journey as I navigate my experience in the foster system and dismantle emotional barriers that went up as a result. Through candid experiences, you'll immerse yourself in my world, experiencing the emotions, struggles, and triumphs firsthand. This memoir format emphasizes facts taken from my own case files, but also includes insights from my younger self. I draw from entries in my Life Book—a repository of memories, milestones, and relationships, which allows me to illuminate past experiences and emotions. After looking at the past, I'll guide you through my current healing process, accompanied by "Seeds of Thought" to help you construct your personal healing journey through reflection. By weaving together these elements, my aim is to create a comprehensive and engaging narrative that encourages you to unburden yourself and confidently walk your own walk.

In embarking on this journey, my primary motivation was to extend a reassuring hand to those who may be struggling. I want you to know that it's okay to leave the past where it belongs until you feel ready to confront it. Through my experiences, I aim to offer comfort and encouragement, reminding you that your own timeline for healing is valid and worthy. May this narrative serve as a source of support and inspiration as you navigate your unique path toward self-discovery and healing.

PART ONE

THE DANDELION'S JOURNEY

PART ONE

THE DANDELION'S JOURNEY

1

EMBARKING

Life in foster care, for me, was like navigating a maze with no end in sight. Each day brought new challenges, new faces, and new uncertainties. But amidst the chaos, there were moments of hope that guided me toward a future I could barely imagine.

Foster care is a system designed for children who cannot reside with their biological parents due to various reasons. These children are placed temporarily in the care of specially trained individuals or families known as foster parents. Ideally, these caregivers create a safe and nurturing environment for the children, while social service agencies work on resolving the issues within the biological family that led to the child's placement.

The primary aim of foster care is to offer children stability and support in a secure environment while actively seeking a permanent home for them. This permanency can be achieved through reunification with their biological family or adoption. Foster care often involves collaboration with various organizations, including nonprofit agencies, community-based organizations, or private providers. These collaborations ensure the delivery of essential services and support to both foster children and families.

The fundamental principles of the foster care system have remained consistent over time. However, reporting data on child welfare outcomes and states' performances in meeting the needs of children became mandatory in 1998 as required by the Adoption and Safe Families Act of 1997 (ASFA). Although data shows progress is being made, especially for youth aging out of foster care, the percentage of these young adults deemed successful remains relatively low. Many aging-out youth, at 18 years old, are left truly on their own, with no support system in place. These challenges lead to staggering outcomes: home-lessness, unemployment, early parenthood, incarceration, and substance use.

Some of the improvements to the foster care system over recent years include enhanced support services for transitioning youth, such as education and employment assistance, mental health support, and housing programs. Additionally, there has been a focus on providing better training and resources for foster parents to create stable and nurturing environments. Moreover, efforts have been made to increase collaboration between social service agencies, nonprofit organizations, and community resources to ensure comprehensive support for both children and families in the system. These improvements aim to enhance the overall well-being and outcomes for children in foster care.

By 1994, I had spent 14 years in the foster care system, and as I aged out of care, I was embarking on a journey filled with independence and uncertainty. My foster home, where I spent the latter part of those years, had been the closest thing to stability I had ever known. With compassion and patience, my foster mother had always been ready to tackle whatever challenges came our way to ensure my well-being. She encouraged me to dream beyond my circumstances, and her unwavering belief in my strength set me on a path out of foster care feeling empowered to take control of my destiny.

One of the pivotal moments that came after foster care for me happened when I was 24 years old. On this day I chose to take a leap of faith and say "yes" to his proposal. A life with him was going to be a dream come true. He embod-ied all I ever wished for in a partner—he was attentive, kind, easygoing, and incredibly supportive. Together, we eagerly anticipated our big day, marking off tasks on the to-do list, including calling the Clerk of Court's office to apply for the marriage license.

The office faxed a three-page marriage license application in preparation for our visit and submission. It was a detailed list of legal requirements to obtain a marriage license, accompanied by a marriage application worksheet. The form required names, addresses, and other details. It's the other details that stirred a mixture of emotions for me. As I began to fill in the spaces for "Father—Name" and "Mother—First and Maiden Name," memories and emotions flooded me. This triggered response was unexpected and I hesitated to continue. I ended up having to call the clerk's office regarding one very specific requirement stating that "each party will need to know their parent's full name, mother's maiden name, and the states in which they were born."

Receptionist (answering the phone): "Thank you for calling the Clerk of Court's office. How may I assist you today?"

Me: "I am calling about #3 on the list of requirements for a Marriage License. Curious, what is the relevance and purpose for parents' names on the application?"

Receptionist: "It is a formality and legal requirement to establish your identity and lineage for legal purposes."

Me: "So, I can not fill in Unknown or Not Applicable."

Receptionist: "No ma'am, you must include this detail on the application and if you have any supporting legal documents, you may submit those as well."

Me: "Hmm, okay, but what if I was a ward . . . ? (Pause.) "Never mind. Thank you for your help."

Receptionist: "You are welcome and remember to please arrive at any of our offices at least 30 minutes prior to closing in order that the application process may be completed."

Me: "Okay, have a nice day."

I discussed the daunting task of completing the application with my fiancé later that day. "'You know I've lived a vastly different life than you," I told him, "and acknowledging my biological parents brings me anxiety. Their names may be on my birth certificate, but that's all they gave me—birth." I expressed my belief that they didn't deserve an acknowledgement in this new chapter of my life. "Believe me," I assured him, "I'm not getting cold feet. It's just a significant life change, and I need a little time to process how I'm going to proceed with completing the form."

In a composed manner, he responded, "I'm sorry you're facing this. We'll proceed with the application whenever you feel prepared."

In the days following, I found myself consumed by the weight of this seemingly simple piece of paper. I grappled with the clash between its legal requirements and its emotional impact. While I knew they were merely asking for a name on a form, for me it held far greater significance. Technically, I had been a ward of the state—a child under the legal guardianship of the government due to my biological parents' inability to care for me. This meant they lacked legal rights, and had left me to navigate childhood and adolescence amidst uncertainty and instability. So, understandably, I harbored strong feelings about identifying them on a legal document that symbolizes love and commitment. This document represented my chance to shed the label of "foster child" and embrace a future brimming with promise.

I went to visit Nancy, my foster mom who I'd lived with for the last seven years I was in the foster care system. Nancy's home was a place where I was always welcomed, and my spontaneous visits seemed to brighten both our days. As I approached her front door, I felt the familiar warmth and comfort that always accompanied my unannounced arrivals.

Entering the house:

"Hey, Nancy, it's me," I called out, breaking the silence that hung in the air.

Nancy turned, her eyes brightening with curiosity. "What brings you here?"

"Just wrapped up with the girls and thought I'd drop by," I replied, a hint of apprehension creeping into my voice.

"Everything alright? How's the wedding planning coming along?" she asked gently.

A heavy sigh escaped me as the weight of my thoughts pressed down on me. "It's the wedding paperwork," I confessed, my voice barely above a whisper. "It's dredging up memories I'd rather forget. It's like I'm held back by the past, unable to move forward."

Nancy's brow raised. "What do you mean, you're grappling with the past?" she murmured, her empathy palpable.

"One of the line items on the marriage license application asks for the parents' name and place of birth. I could easily fill it out from my birth certificate, but it's like every bit of joy is overshadowed by the pain of my past. I feel trapped, denied happiness."

"You've faced so much adversity, you're stronger than you realize," Nancy reassured me. "Your experience and determination have shaped you into the resilient person you are. Completing this form should remind you of that strength, not hold you back. Don't allow the outside noise to derail your future."

Tears pricked at my eyes as her words washed over me, "You're right," I whispered, "but I do not know if I can consciously put the ink on paper."

A moment of silence passed between us, the air heavy with unspoken words. "Brandy," she began, her voice filled with emotion, "there's something I've been meaning to ask you and was waiting for a perfect time."

My heart quickened as I waited for her next words, sensing the gravity of the moment.

"I want to officially adopt you," Nancy declared, her eyes shining with determination. "To solidify our bond and affirm the family we've created together. We can make the adoption official before the wedding. This way, you can proceed with the marriage license."

Shock and gratitude surged through me, leaving me speechless for a moment. "Really? Can we do that? I'm an adult."

"Absolutely," Nancy replied, her confidence unwavering. "You're an adult, so the process is straightforward and quick."

I stammered, overcome with emotion. "I . . . I don't know what to say."

Nancy reached out and squeezed my hand gently. "You don't have to say anything now. Just know that you'll always have a place in my heart, no matter what."

In that moment, as warmth flooded my being, I knew that I was truly home.

Nancy, deeply connected within the community, wasted no time initiating the adoption process. In a matter of weeks, we found ourselves sitting across from a family law attorney, navigating the intricacies of filing a petition at the courthouse for adoption. Given the straightforward nature of our case and its uncontested status, we found ourselves on a path toward an informal and private adoption proceeding that would take place within the solemn chambers of a judge.

Filled with anticipation and hope, we arrived at the designated courthouse, ready to embark on the next chapter of our journey. With a stack of necessary documents in hand, we stepped into the hallowed halls of justice, eager to formalize the bond that had already taken root in our hearts.

As we stood before the judge, I couldn't help but feel a sense of apprehension mingled with excitement. With minimal small talk, the judge delved into the procedural legalities, his demeanor professional and precise.

"Do you understand the responsibilities and legal obligations that come with adoption?" he inquired, his voice echoing in the solemn chamber.

With each question, the weight of the moment grew heavier. The gravity of our decision hung in the air like a delicate thread. And then, with a final nod of acknowledgment, the judge delivered his verdict.

"Based on the consent of all parties, I find that this adult adoption is in the best interest of those involved. I will issue an adoption decree finalizing this adoption. Congratulations to you both."

Relief washed over us like a tidal wave, mingled with the joy that bubbled up from deep within our souls. "Thank you, your honor," we murmured in unison, our voices filled with gratitude and emotion.

As we embraced each other tightly, I whispered, "I'm so happy to officially be family."

The judge, his gaze softening with understanding, offered a parting sentiment. "It's obvious this means a great deal for you both. I'm not sure of your path to get here, but happy you found each other."

With his words lingering in the air like a benediction, we stepped out of the courthouse, our hearts light and spirits lifted. For in that sacred chamber of justice, amidst the formalities and legalities, we found not just validation, but the affirmation of a bond that transcended bloodlines and legal documents. We were declared family.

2

FRAGMENTS OF LIFE

In my 30s, I found myself standing before a Memory Box. Time had marched on, and life had taken unexpected turns, yet the contents within remained unchanged, frozen in time like artifacts of an era. The label on the weathered box read, "Brandy childhood memories," a simple yet profound declaration of its contents. While such boxes are typically lovingly curated by parents, mine was a catchall for everything related to my upbringing—a tangible archive of my life.

Receiving the Memory Box from Nancy, who meticulously saved everything, felt like I'd inherited a treasure trove of memories, yet I hesitated to delve into its depths. The thought of revisiting the past filled me with unease, as if opening the box would unleash a whirlwind of conflicting emotions I wasn't ready to confront. Adopting Eleanor Roosevelt's mantra, "Yesterday is history, tomorrow is a mystery, today is a gift," I focused on that moment rather than dwelling on the ghosts of the past. It was a conscious effort to embrace the here and now, to appreciate each moment as it came without being burdened by yesterday's baggage.

Despite having embraced the philosophy of living in the present, I couldn't shake the feeling that the box held secrets waiting to be unearthed—stories that longed to be told, perhaps with vital information. I stood at a crossroads and took a deep breath. I prepared myself for a brief delve into the box, intending to swiftly extract the information needed.

As I lifted the lid, a rush of nostalgia flooded over me. Faded clothing laid on top and held memories like time capsules, each piece whispered stories of adventures long past. Among them, the worn black Poison T-shirt stood out, evoking memories of my headbanging days filled with loud music, big hair, and grunge attire. Its presence in the Memory Box brought a smirk to my lips, a reminder of a rebellious era filled with youthful energy.

Also inside the box, I found my Life Book, a testament to my early years. Measuring 11.5 by 12 inches, this hardcover brown leather book was packed with sentiments. Each photograph, scribble, and handwritten entry was a fragment of my past, capturing moments both joyful and fraught with fear. The yellowed pages overflowed with the raw emotions of my younger self, serving as a poignant reminder of the journey I had traveled and the resilience I had shown along the way.

As I continued to sift through the familiar items, my fingers brushed against the adoption decree, its significance now more profound than ever before. I imagined Nancy, the woman who had welcomed me into her heart and home, carefully placing it inside the box, recognizing it as a symbol of our bond, a testament to the hardships and triumphs that had brought us together.

The bundle of personal cards and letters inside the Memory Box carried the voices of those who accompanied me on my journey. Though the ink had slightly blurred with time, the sentiments expressed within resonated deeply, offering glimpses into the connections forged and the support received along the way. Each card and letter was a cherished reminder of the impact others have had on my life.

And then there were the photographs, frozen moments of laughter, tears, and everything in between, each one a chapter in the story of who I became. As I poked through the contents of the box, I couldn't help but feel a sense of heartache. Each item held a story, a memory, a piece of my identity. Despite the familiarity of the contents, the feelings were raw and overwhelming—sadness and sorrow mingled with uncertainty as I struggled with the prospect of reliving painful memories. Yet, driven by the necessity of my quest, I pushed forward, skimming the pages of the Life Book and the contents of the Memory Box alike.

I turned my focus to a set of bound documents. I hoped to find the answers that led me to open the Memory Box, the answers about family medical history. However, my search yielded little beyond routine immunizations and physical examinations, leaving me frustrated and no closer to understanding my genetic makeup or medical history. Yet, amidst the disappointment, a discovery caught my eye: a "Child's Face Sheet," a relic of my past that served as a window into the myriad places I had called home. Each entry represented a chapter of my life, a reminder of the faces and places that shaped my journey. As I studied the photograph of a young child smiling up at me, I was struck by the stark contrast between appearance and reality. Behind that innocent smile was a world of untold struggles and hardships. It was a poignant reminder of the disconnect between outward perception and inner turmoil, of the masks I wore to conceal my pain from the world. I gazed at the photograph, and couldn't help but wonder about the child behind the smile, about the battles fought and the scars left behind. It was a moment of introspection, a reminder that the truth of an experience often lies hidden beneath the surface, waiting to be uncovered and understood.

As I navigated the emotional storm unleashed by delving into the Memory Box, I realized I wasn't yet ready to confront the painful mysteries of my past. The anxiety and fear it stirred threatened to overshadow my present peace, prompting a conscious decision to prioritize my emotional well-being. With resolve, I pushed the contents back into the box, refusing to let it steal my joy. I contemplated renaming it "Pandora's Box," with its potential to stir up negativity and unresolved emotions. I chose to set it aside and grant myself permission to leave the painful information tucked away for another day. Having survived trauma, I questioned the necessity of risking a revisit to that pain. I chose to honor the wisdom of timing, knowing that the past would still be waiting for me when the moment was right.

Looking through the Memory Box, another curiosity had emerged—a longing to uncover the identity of my biological father. This question had lingered since childhood. Over the years, not knowing had become more significant, urging me to embark on the daunting yet potentially liberating journey of discovery. The contents of the Memory Box resonated with this longing, igniting a desire to be brave and confront the unknown. Would this be the moment to take that leap, to seek the answers I'd yearned for for so long?

Months passed before I mustered the courage to embark on the journey of finding my biological father, knowing it wasn't a decision to take lightly. Armed with determination, I reached out to individuals who might have information, seeking guidance from supportive figures like Nancy, who proved instrumental throughout the process. With their help, I was connected with a family reunification specialist who guided me through the careful process of embracing patience and managing expectations. Once I decided to move forward, a private investigator was brought in to locate my biological father. Since his information was on my birth certificate and he was military, the process was relatively straightforward due to his extensive paper trail. Within a couple of weeks, the private investigator returned with a comprehensive file that included contact information, current photos, and details about what appeared to be other family members living with him.

The specialist reviewed the file with me, coaching me through the initial contact stage and discussing how to approach it. She ensured I was fully aware of my options and confirmed that this was truly what I still wanted to do. I had the choice to set the information aside and revisit it when I felt ready. After a week of deliberation, I decided to take the plunge and make contact.

The initial contact didn't go as anticipated, or at least not how I had scripted it in my head. I wasn't entirely sure what to expect, but I hadn't prepared for his reservations. His first question was, "How do I know you are truly who you say you are?" A fair question, considering the circumstances. After I proved my identity, he admitted that, in the back of his mind, he had always known this day might come.

Our early conversations were marked by apprehension, long pauses, and nervous laughter. Navigating our reunion proved to be both challenging and complex, despite the initial promise it held. It was a whirlwind, but his presence filled a void I hadn't fully realized was there—a sense of someone claiming me as their own. Yet, intertwined with the warmth and affection, there was a profound sadness reminding me of the years lost and the mourning for the time that had slipped away. Frustration found its place in our journey, particularly when he failed to acknowledge his role in my distorted childhood. My father's absence from my childhood hung in the air whenever we communicated or got together, and the weight of his abandonment clouded my mind, creating an unspoken barrier between us.

In our limited heartfelt conversations, there was a sense of unease whenever the conversation veered too close to the topic of his absence. It felt like we were both tiptoeing around, afraid of the emotional toll that would ensue if we went down that road. Questions lingered in my mind—why had he let me go? Did he ever think of me? Why didn't he come looking for me? How could he live a comfortable life without me in it? But the fear of opening up old wounds and disrupting an already fragile bond kept those questions locked away. They were unspoken yet ever present.

As time passed, I couldn't help but wonder if one day we would find the courage to address the unspoken pain, to unravel the layers of the "whys" and "hows." Until then, I conditioned myself to accept what it was and what I had been given as a coping mechanism. It was a conscious choice, a survival strategy that allowed me to navigate the limitations of our newfound father-daughter relationship. Instead of dwelling on what could have been, I focused on the present moment. But I never felt comfortable with the unknown truth, and I couldn't erase my curiosity. I had a desire for a deeper authentic connection—a bond where we could truly understand, trust, and relate to each other. But would I ever be brave enough to get there?

3

NAVIGATING LIFE'S TERRAIN

Despite the complexities with my father, one particular event brought profound blessings into our relationship—when I attended his mother's (my grandmother's) funeral. As I made the decision to travel to the small town of my father's childhood for the funeral, I was met with a mix of anticipation, fear, and a heavy heart. The prospect of unfamiliar faces and being surrounded by grief left me apprehensive, but I knew it was a journey I was capable of making.

I reeled in my unease, packed my bags, and embarked on the eight-hour trip to the memorial. Each mile brought a flood of thoughts and questions—how would I be introduced to everyone? Did I belong? These uncertainties weighed heavily on my mind. Adding to my apprehension was the knowledge that my father had been absent from his home and family for decades, with no close ties to any relatives.

Arriving at the funeral home, I decided just to observe, quietly taking in the somber atmosphere. Soon, despite my best intentions, I found myself facing introductions and engaging in conversations with my father's relatives. Each introduction was met with butterflies. Would I be introduced as his daughter? Yes, yes I would. I was greeted with warm welcomes. There was an eagerness from them to learn all about me. These encounters triggered a wave of responses—surprise, hurt, and an overwhelming sense of loss. I struggled to compose myself, and excused myself to seek relief outside from my intense emotional state.

Gasping for air, I felt a surge of shock wash over me as I realized each person in the room had been aware of my existence before I'd arrived. The weight of this revelation felt suffocating, and I began to experience symptoms of a panic attack. With my eyes closed, I focused on taking deep, steady breaths, attempting to regain control over my racing thoughts and the overwhelming physical response. As I breathed deeply, I allowed myself to acknowledge the ache of being known but not being rescued. With each breath, I found a glimmer of strength, a determination to face the situation head-on. Steadying my trembling body, I wiped the tears from my face and composed myself.

Summoning all the courage within me, I walked back into the room, ready to confront whatever conversations awaited me. Despite the turmoil raging within me, I had to find the strength to navigate this challenging moment with grace and resilience.

In the midst of this emotional rollercoaster, I met a man who shared a unique connection to my biological parents. He was my father's childhood friend and military buddy, and he had been present during the first few months of my life, witnessing my first physical bonds, cries, and smiles. As he shared glimpses into my past and stories of the good old days, it became surreal. Hearing about these pivotal moments from a complete stranger added another layer of complexity to my already tumultuous state of mind.

As guests left the funeral home, I found myself receiving requests for my contact information from family members—a gesture that filled me with both apprehension and hope. With cautious optimism, I exchanged information, opening the door to the possibility of forging deep-rooted and intense connections.

That night, as I lay in bed, the weight of the day's encounters lingered in my mind. The thought of the graveside gathering the next day filled me with uncertainty as I braced myself for what awaited me.

The next day, sitting in the cemetery, perched atop a peaceful hill with serene landscaping and breathtaking views, my mood pressed heavily upon me. Surrounded by the silent presence of the graveyard, I found myself engulfed in deep thoughts about my past and my roots. Each gravestone seemed to whisper stories of lives once lived, triggering memories and emotions that flooded my heart. With each passing moment, the ache in my heart grew deeper, and I yearned for respite from it all. The burden of my past was an unbearable weight, one that I struggled to carry alone. In that moment of solitude, I longed for a sanctuary where I could unburden my soul and find understanding amidst the chaos in my mind. In the quiet atmosphere of the cemetery, I found myself silently pleading with the heavens above, reaching out to God for relief. "Make this stop," I whispered. "I do not want to do this. I am alone in my struggle." It was a moment of raw vulnerability, a desperate plea for comfort in the midst of overwhelming pain.

After the internment, I treaded softly along a path, each step a deliberate effort to maintain composure amidst the whirlwind of the moment and of all the new "family." With my eyes fixed on the markers, I contemplated the significance of this moment. With every stride, I breathed deeply, using the act of walking as a form of meditation to calm the noise in my head and navigate through the turbulent moment.

Suddenly, a gentle touch on my shoulder broke the solitude. It was Mabel, a cousin I had met the night before. "I can't imagine what you're feeling," she said softly, "but if you'd like, I can walk with you and point out family markers." We linked arms, her gentle touch reassuring, as we embarked on this journey together. As we walked, she wove a narrative of our lineage, speaking of ancestors with pride and sharing stories of their struggles, achievements, and legacies passed down through generations.

Listening intently, my heart swelled with a sense of belonging—each marker representing a chapter of our family history. I began to see more than just inscriptions on cold marble; I saw the incredible strength and resilience that bound us together as a family. Guided by Mabel's loving hand and the stories of generations past, I felt a part of a rich family heritage—a family tree connected by traditions, values, and shared experiences.

A glimmer of hope flickered within me here among the gravestones—in such an unusual and unexpected place to find peace. After 42 years of carrying the burden of my childhood and longing to belong, I had discovered a piece of my identity and strength. Finally, I felt able to breathe. A seed of connection was planted—a seed that held the possibility of building lasting and meaningful relationships with newfound family members.

As I began the long drive home following the emotional roller coaster of the funeral events, the car became my sanctuary. With each passing mile, the anger that coursed through me became more palpable, fueled by the profound sense of being robbed—robbed of the chance to grow up with the family I had only just discovered. It was a gut-wrenching realization, a bitter pill to swallow, knowing that I had missed out on years of familial guidance and the warmth of unconditional love.

Each mile on the road amplified this injustice, magnifying the enormity of what had been stolen from me. I couldn't help but envision the childhood I could have had—where I would have played, attended school, gone to church—all of which had been denied through a twist of fate and a veil of secrets. I raged against the unfairness of growing up without this support, having to navigate the complexities of life alone.

In the solitude of my car, my hands clenched the steering wheel as fury stirred inside. Questions echoed in my mind, demanding answers from the universe. How could my parents abandon me? Why did it have to be this way? Tears mingled with fury, a turbulent mix of sadness and resentment. The road ahead stretched endlessly, my heart heavy with the longing for clarity and resolution.

With a heavy heart, I reached for my phone and dialed the number of my dearest friend and mentor. As she answered with a simple, "Hey," a rush of emotions swept over me. There was no time for formalities; I needed her to hear the raw truth of my heart. "I can't hold it in anymore," I confessed, my voice trembling with emotion. "I'm angry, I'm sad, and I feel like I'm drowning in all of it. And honestly, I hate my mother for what she did, and I want to confront her." I know hate is a strong word, but at this moment it was the only one that seemed to fit.

As I poured out my tangled thoughts and feelings, she listened with understanding. She reminded me I was more than my circumstances, that it was okay to feel overwhelmed. Her words were a lifeline, grounding me in the midst of despair.

"You don't have to figure it all out right now," she reassured me. "Give yourself the grace to process. Take one step at a time."

During our conversation, I began to feel a sense of clarity. Her words inspired me to channel my emotions into something meaningful. As we said our goodbyes, her suggestion lingered in my mind. Maybe it was time to start writing that book, to turn my pain into something inspiring.

As I continued my drive, I felt a shift within me. I spoke aloud to myself about my encounters with a newfound family so I could embrace the complexity of it all. I couldn't shake the feeling that there was a deeper significance to this experience. Was it conceivable that God orchestrated this profound experience to prompt me to acknowledge, value, and cherish the essence of my existence?

Hours later, my phone buzzed with a Facebook Messenger notification. Opening the app, I found a heartfelt message from cousin Kiki. Her words struck a chord within me as she expressed, "It is sad you had no idea how much you were loved and thought about all these years. If Mammaw, your great-grandmother, were still with us, she would have held you forever. In fact, Mammaw kept your birth announcement from the newspaper in her Bible and she wanted your dad to bring you home." All the way home from the funeral, cousin Kib had expressed similar sentiments, saying, "I had always wondered what happened to that little girl."

Carefully navigating the delicate balance of warmth and caution, I remained mindful of the feelings that had already surfaced—the anger, the sadness, and the need for self-protection. As messages and emails began connecting me to relatives one by one, I gradually found myself letting go of all of them, bringing down the walls around my heart. With each exchange, previous apprehensions became a beacon of hope and I found the courage to embrace the future.

Their stories wove together into a larger narrative, one I was eager to explore. Fifteen months later, I returned to my father's hometown and connected with a bustling newfound family. It was a courageous leap into the unknown. The whole clan of cousins welcomed me with warmth and excitement, making me feel instantly accepted. As I stepped into their homes, I felt like a rock star or some-one of great importance, embraced and celebrated in ways I never imagined.

Among the shared stories and laughter, I was gifted a tangible piece of my past—my birth announcement. Kiki enlisted a friend at the newspaper to find it in the archives. Holding the framed announcement in my hands, I felt the love Mammaw would have shown me. The birth announcement, adorned with my baby picture, name, and birth date, became a tangible link to my identity. It symbolized the welcome I would have received coming into the world by my family. This simple yet profound artifact was more than just a document; it was a piece of my story, marking the beginning of my journey and how far I had come. I traced my fingers over its words and felt a deep sense of belonging. It was a gesture that went beyond words—a reminder I was not just a newcomer in their lives, but a long-awaited family member.

Cousin Kib, known for his storytelling finesse, orchestrated a day of explora-tion that opened up the town's rich history. As we wandered through its quaint streets, each corner seemed to whisper tales of generations past. He painted scenes of simple joys and a close-knit family bound by strong values and bonds. It was a day brimming with newfound knowledge and cherished memories. Saying goodbye that weekend, I felt deeply rooted and connected, as if a miss-ing piece of my identity had finally fallen into place.

Returning home, I realized this journey had not only enriched my life but also sparked a deeper sense of curiosity. While the birth announcement may have brought joy to some, for me it served as a reminder of a tumultuous start in life. I wondered if this recent experience was a sign to unravel the circumstances of my childhood and gain a deeper understanding of my identity and past. Would this journey offer closure and help me reconcile the challenges I had faced?

After years of hesitation and brushing it aside, I could no longer ignore the pull—it was time. Time to delve deep into the depths of my past, piecing together the fragments of identity amidst the uncertainty that clouded my childhood. Growing up, I found myself adrift in a sea of nameless emotions, drowning in a tide of confusion and pain. To cope, I buried those feelings deep within, shielding myself from the rawness of my reality. But beneath the surface, the wounds festered, leaving scars on my soul that no one could see. Trust became a rare commodity, and I navigated the world like a lone sailor, wary of every wave that threatened to engulf me.

Yet, despite the darkness that loomed over my past, this day felt different. I stood at the threshold of my own healing, ready to confront the shadows that had haunted me for so long. It wouldn't be an easy journey—I knew there would be tears, fears, and moments of doubt. But I was on a mission to reclaim my story and to rewrite the narrative of my life with courage and resilience at its core. So away I went, diving deep back into the Memory Box!

With each memory unearthed, I gained clarity and understanding. I refused to let my struggles define me; instead, I embraced them as part of my journey, as stepping stones to a brighter future. By acknowledging my pain and facing it head-on, I took back control of my narrative, steering it toward a path of healing and wholeness. In that journey, I found my true strength—not just in the challenges I overcame, but in my unwavering commitment to seek resolution and find peace within myself.

Although this heartfelt journey is raw and intense, there's a shared understanding that we all experience seasons of hardships. So, regardless of the season you're facing, I invite you to walk alongside me on a path of hope and healing. While we may not see what lies ahead, every step taken in hope brings us closer to embracing healing.

With each obstacle we overcome, we forge a future defined by courage, strength, and enduring peace. Every challenge conquered brings us closer to a life where resilience is second nature and hope lights our path. In this journey, we build a legacy of determination and unwavering faith, ensuring that every step forward is a testament to our growth and perseverance. So let's journey forward together, supporting and uplifting each other along the way.

⤜ Seeds of Vulnerability ⤛

Reflecting on the themes of your past can be a deeply personal journey. Embracing the readiness to resolve the pain is a powerful step toward healing and personal growth. It signifies your inner strength and determination to overcome the wounds of the past. As you delve into the depths of your struggles and confront the pain, remember that this process is a testament to your resilience. Acknowledge the hurt, allow yourself to feel, and then channel that energy into positive actions and self-care. With time, patience, and self-compassion, you can transform the pain into wisdom, strength, and a deeper understanding of yourself. Healing is a journey, and you demonstrate incredible courage by taking the first steps toward resolution. Celebrate every small victory along the way, and above all, be kind and patient with yourself. Healing is a gradual process, and it's okay to have setbacks. What matters most is your determination to keep moving forward. Keep believing in yourself, and you will achieve the peace and healing you deserve.

Reflective seeds, like this, are scattered throughout this memoir to serve as prompts for contemplation on your healing journey. They offer thoughtful considerations to address unresolved pain associated with trauma or past experiences. I put "Seeds of Vulnerability" first, since I find that it's a crucial initial step for beginning.

Embarking on this healing journey demands acknowledging the power of vulnerability. It is the pivotal first step—a willingness to unveil one's true self, complete with emotional struggles and scars. Opening up in this way allows for authentic connections, fostering understanding and empathy. Honest self-reflection becomes possible, enabling a deeper understanding of the wounds in need of healing.

The key here is to approach vulnerability with caution. It's essential to establishing a safe and supportive environment where discussing your experiences fosters healing. Finding the right space, though it may require careful navigation, can lead to significant changes in how you cope with, and comprehend, the lasting effects of past traumas. Vulnerability becomes an avenue for emotional expression, releasing pent-up feelings and promoting emotional well-being. It demands courage, pushing you beyond your comfort zones toward personal growth.

Writing about your experiences can provide a safe space for vulnerability because it allows you to express thoughts and emotions without fear of immediate judgment. It can help you process and understand your feelings, leading to self-awareness and personal growth. Additionally, sharing your experiences through writing can create connections with others who may relate or offer support, fostering a sense of community and understanding.

Traumatic experiences often breed isolation, but vulnerability shatters those barriers, reminding individuals that they are not alone in their struggles. Sharing vulnerabilities can build trust and strengthen relationships, creating a safe space for healing. Moreover, it challenges the notion that you need to hide imperfections, fostering self-acceptance on the healing journey.

Admittedly, vulnerability used to be incredibly uncomfortable for me, driven by the fear of reopening wounds and sinking into emotional despair. My stark reality has been that one's significance is often tied to public visibility. While I've been acknowledged as a success and survivor by those acquainted with my story, not being completely comfortable with myself led to missed opportunities to advocate for change. Despite possessing valuable knowledge and experiences, my reluctance to share them widely has resulted in being overlooked, essentially being perceived as not relevant. It's an unfortunate truth I wrestle with, acknowledging that my hesitation stems from the fear of retraumatizing myself. I used to justify my silence by irrationally downplaying my experiences, convinced they were insignificant compared to others' trauma. This limited perspective, rooted in the only life I knew, would hinder me from making a broader impact.

For a considerable time, the idea of writing a book felt daunting, as it meant laying bare my vulnerabilities. The fear of judgment and pity, coupled with the desire to maintain the comfort of my current life without drawing attention to my imperfections, held me back. However, over time and by digging deep within, I came to realize that the strength I would gain through sharing my story outweighed the potential discomfort.

I've come to understand that vulnerability, when approached mindfully and within a supportive environment, can serve as a powerful tool against retraumatization. Opening up and sharing your experiences, which might seem challenging, surprisingly weakens the impact of past traumas. It's like a step-by-step process, gradually making the emotional weight of those memories lighter. Keep in mind, it's not a quick fix, but more of a journey toward feeling less affected by the past.

Every passing day brings a subtle transformation—I sense a gradual lightening, as if a heavy weight is lifted from the healing process. The growing lightness feels like a refreshing breath of air, infusing a newfound hope into each of my tomorrows. It's a great lesson I've learned—acknowledging and addressing the pain of the past can pave the way for a brighter, more hopeful, and more peaceful future.

Reflection

As you go further into your own healing journey, ponder what healing means to you. How do you define it in your own life? How have your past experiences influenced your present perspective on life?

As you consider the role of vulnerability in the healing journey, ask yourself: What fears or hesitations have held you back? Reflect on instances in your life where being open and genuine with others, or even with yourself, has led to a deeper sense of connection, understanding, and personal growth. How might embracing vulnerability shape your healing journey and self-discovery?

To explore vulnerability, try these activities:

Vulnerability Journal Start a journal where you reflect on moments when you felt vulnerable. Write about the emotions, thoughts, and experiences associated with those moments.

Artistic Expression Express vulnerability through creative mediums such as writing, painting, or music. Use art as a means of processing and expressing your emotions.

Role-Playing Exercise Practice being vulnerable by engaging in role-playing scenarios with a trusted friend or therapist. Experiment with expressing your feelings and asking for support or understanding.

Vulnerability Challenge Set a personal challenge to step out of your comfort zone and embrace vulnerability in a specific area of your life. This could involve initiating a difficult conversation, sharing a personal story publicly, or asking for help when needed.

PART TWO

A FRAGILE BEGINNING

4

BONDS UNRAVELED—THE BIOLOGICAL FAMILY

*My name is Brandy. I have dirty blonde hair and blue eyes. I don't remember
anything about my father. I know he was very tall. My parents were married but
they did not get along very well. They separated and my mother and I came back
to her hometown. The social worker says my mom did not like my dad too much
& that she kind of let that interfere with her liking me—because I was my dad's
daughter. That wasn't very fair of her. Anyway, we came back & I was growing
and learning to talk. My mother met my stepfather & they got married.
They had a child together. By then I could run & hop.
It was a lot of fun to have a sibling.*

We got along very, very good.

Life Book Entry, August 1981

Case Summary, 1981

The mother contacted the Division of Health and Human Resources, requesting foster care for her daughter, Brandy. Following her call, she visited the agency's office to formalize her request. The mother, recently separated from her husband, attributed the tension in her relationship to Brandy. She expressed financial inability to support Brandy and questioned her love for her daughter, suggesting her negative feelings toward Brandy's biological father influenced her bond. The mother openly criticized Brandy's appearance, citing her obesity, and complained about Brandy's behavior, including refusal to do schoolwork, lying, and stealing. Brandy's stepfather expressed strong dislike for her and issued an ultimatum to the mother, who chose her husband over Brandy in a bid to salvage her marriage, showing little concern for the child's welfare.

Brandy, a six-year-old girl with blonde hair and blue eyes, lives with her biological mother, stepfather, and half-sibling in a comfortable two-story home. Her mother, who is self-employed, met Brandy's biological father during their military service, but they separated soon after Brandy's birth. The mother moved back to her hometown, where she remarried and had another child. Brandy's biological father has not been involved in her life and has provided inconsistent support.

⇒╪╪⇐

T he tactile sensation of old paper evokes a cascade of emotions and
memories.

Life at home with my biological mom and stepfather had meant
tiptoeing through a minefield of explosive anger and cruelty. Each day was a
silent battle filled with discomfort and fear, never knowing what would trigger
the next outburst. It wasn't always chaos, but calm moments were few. As I witnessed my mother's suffering, I too experienced the horrors of aggression and
violence. My mother and stepfather directed their hostility of emotional, physical, and sexual abuse toward me. I spent most of my time in my bedroom, lonely
and scared. Often, I was left alone with my stepfather while my mother worked,
and on those days, I didn't mind being locked up and neglected. His attitude
was clear: "Not my kid; not my responsibility." Nothing good ever came from
our interactions. When he did approach me, an unsettling feeling would wash
over me. I knew what was coming. He'd lead me to the bedroom, always reminding me of our secret, and the danger of telling anyone. I was all too familiar with
this routine, so I would close my eyes and brace myself.

I distinctly remember on one given day my mother arriving home unexpectedly, disrupting his diabolical actions. In response, he violently attacked her,
beating her mercilessly while I curled into a ball on the bed, fearing I would be
next. The onslaught felt endless until he finally fled, leaving a chilling silence
behind. My mother, bloodied and battered, stumbled toward me, embracing
me in silence. In that moment, her love for me had been painfully evident.

The constant reminder of abuse was inescapable. At school, a watchful adult
regularly inquired about my home life, leaving me wondering if she sensed the
hidden chaos. I faked a smile, nodded, and gave vague responses, desperate
to hide the torment within. Returning home after the probing questions was
agonizing. Inside, the air was heavy with tension, and I faced more restrictions—
locked away and forbidden to speak to anyone, ever.

In the depths of isolation, I endured relentless separation from the family.
Countless hours passed within the confines of my bedroom, hunger gnawed at
my stomach, and fear gripped my heart. Whenever someone approached the
door, panic would wash over me, a feeling of dread as to who waited on the
other side. In moments of despair, I contemplated whether the crushing loneliness was preferable to the potential cruelty beyond that door. Little did I know,

my freedom would arrive in a way I had never anticipated, reshaping my world unexpectedly and drastically.

On a particular summer day, everything seemed ordinary at first glance. Yet, as the hours passed, an unsettling feeling started to linger, particularly noticeable in my mother's increasingly distant and cold demeanor. My unease intensified when I discovered my belongings gathered near the front door, a silent precursor to impending change. The tension eventually reached its peak when a knock echoed through the house. As my mother answered the door, I was introduced to a stranger whose familiarity with the situation surpassed my understanding. This flow of events led to my abrupt and bewildering departure from the only home I had ever known. My mother's silence spoke volumes as she stood by, offering no explanation or comfort. Tears streaked down my cheeks and I pleaded desperately to stay, clinging to the familiar, but my cries fell on deaf ears. As the car pulled away from the curb, my heart heavy with confusion and fear, I watched my mother's figure fade into the distance, a silent shift of the life I would soon learn I was leaving behind.

When I entered an office building, individuals who introduced themselves as social workers attempted to reassure me that everything would be okay. The words, "Your mother asked for our help because she cannot take care of you," reverberated emptily in my mind, shattering the illusion of a mother's unconditional love. I trembled with fear and tears blurred my vision. I retreated inward, yearning to escape the nightmare engulfing my reality. Despite the social worker's gentle prodding for conversation, the responses I gave were fractured, clouded by a whirlpool of confusion and self-blame. I felt I was being punished for the secrets hidden behind those closed doors, the horrors I dared not speak about. Flashbacks flooded my mind, blurring the line between reality and nightmare. They left me stranded in a world where trust was a distant memory and safety a fragile illusion. The uncertain road ahead loomed darkly, each passing moment a stark reminder of shattered innocence and fractured trust. It all shaped my journey forward.

⇥ Seeds of Empathy ⇤

Understanding empathy and its significance in the healing process can be challenging yet essential, especially for survivors of abuse or trauma. Empathy involves stepping into someone else's shoes, experiencing the world from their perspective, and recognizing their state of mind. Cultivating empathy is invaluable for the healing process for several reasons.

First, it helps survivors understand that the abuse was not their fault, easing self-blame and guilt. Second, it creates connections with others who share similar experiences, fostering a supportive community. Additionally, empathy promotes self-compassion, enabling victims to be kind to themselves, a crucial aspect of healing. By empathizing, survivors can break the cycle of abuse and nurture healthier relationships.

Moreover, practicing empathy assists survivors in processing and expressing their emotions and facilitating their healing journey. Being empathetic toward others as they share provides valuable insights into our own experiences, helping us to make sense of our trauma and move toward recovery. Reflecting on someone's history and struggles doesn't excuse their actions, but it offers a glimpse into their complex battles and the factors that led to their behavior.

For me, empathy had a transformative impact on my own experience. I initially found it counterproductive, as it was emotionally draining trying to understand and accommodate the bitterness I carried. But becoming empathetic proved to be a powerful step in my journey.

As an adult, I naturally empathize with individuals who have not directly caused me harm. It's not a forced quality, but something I inherited through my life's experiences. Turning this tendency inward, I visualized people from my past differently; I stopped looking at them as a threat. I took the courageous step of seeking understanding of those who had caused me harm. Although it was challenging at first, I gradually became more comfortable with this practice.

Instead of looking solely at the hurt my mother caused me, or the harm that befell me in her home, I started to find myself curious about the underlying intentions that guided her actions and allegiance. It was clear my mother suffered from domestic violence too, but was her upbringing in a similar environment? Did she ever experience anything different to know an alternative way of life?

I allow myself to wrestle with other questions that might have impacted the way others acted toward me, such as: Why do some people harm children? What factors increase the risk of abusing a child? Seeking understanding, I explore these queries. Surprisingly, uncovering trauma in another's past, though it won't excuse their behavior fully, can provide insight to help me find empathy.

Recognizing that the behavior of others was influenced by external pressures, past experiences, and internal struggles has helped me realize their actions weren't solely about me. It provides me with the emotional distance I need to move forward.

By considering these factors and empathizing, I am able to understand their perspective, but on my terms. Reclaiming control over the narrative empowers me, shifting the balance of power and allowing me to see their circumstance from a position of strength. Humanizing them helps me let go of intense negativity, anger, and resentment and frees me from the hold the trauma has had. While acknowledging my pain, I realize what I endured wasn't my fault, which makes room for self-compassion.

Reflection

No matter how chaotic, reflecting on one's history is a vital part of personal growth. Reflecting on the importance of empathy in healing, consider these questions: What role does empathy play in connecting with your experiences, especially those involving adversity? How might cultivating empathy help you better understand your own emotions and experiences? Are there situations in which you find it challenging to empathize with others? What can you do to overcome those challenges? In what ways do you currently practice empathy in your relationships and interactions with others?

Explore how empathy and understanding might bridge gaps in your relationships. Think about a difficult occurrence in your life. How would you feel if others approached your struggles with empathy and a desire to understand?

Reflect on the power of empathy in fostering resilience. How does understanding others' struggles inspire hope and determination?

To cultivate empathy, try these activities:

Perspective-Taking Exercise Choose a person in your life and try to see the world from their perspective for a day. Reflect on their experiences, emotions, and challenges.

Stranger Interview Approach someone you don't know well and ask them about their life experiences, interests, and dreams. Practice active listening and empathetic engagement during the conversation.

Empathy Journal Keep a journal where you write about moments when you felt deeply connected to someone else's emotions or experiences. Reflect on what you learned from these encounters.

Volunteer Work Engage in volunteer activities that allow you to interact with people from different backgrounds or those facing challenges. This could be at a homeless shelter, nursing home, or community center.

Media Analysis Choose a movie, book, or news article that explores themes of empathy and analyze how characters or real-life individuals demonstrate empathy toward others.

5

SHELTERED—THE FOSTER FAMILY

While I was living with my mom, my stepfather, and sibling, things were not good. He did not like me because I was not his natural child. Things with my real mom were not good either. She was upset with me because he did not like me. That wasn't my fault. Sometimes a stepfamily can be very difficult and hard. It is the parents' job to help children make adjustments to the family. My mom and stepfather didn't do their job. I like my sibling a lot though. We were good friends. My mother gave me to the state. She said she didn't want me in the family anymore. That hurt and I cried for a long time. Now I am beginning to learn that wasn't my fault. I was only six years old. My mother did not know how to take care of me and her marriage too.

I get very angry when I think about it.

Life Book Entry, March 1983

Case Summary, 1983

Brandy was placed in foster care 11 days after her mother's initial contact with the state agency, following a voluntary agreement signed by her mother. The state intended to declare her a "child in need of care" due to her mother's inability and unwillingness to care for her. Brandy's mother was agreeable and opted out of a court hearing, expressing eagerness to part ways with the child.

Brandy, an active and chubby child, was taken in by an older couple in their mid-50s. The foster parents, who had raised their own children, declared they were dedicated to providing love and support for Brandy. The foster mother was outspoken and involved in the community, while the foster father, nurturing and simple, embodied a grandfatherly figure.

Brandy, deeply distressed by her placement, longed for reconciliation with her mother. Plans involved continuing foster care, obtaining psychiatric and physical examinations for Brandy, and arranging visits with her mother, with the possibility of reuniting them. Brandy's experiences at school revealed her past struggles, including hunger and a need for affection. Reports from other parents indicated physical abuse and mistreatment at her mother's home, where she was made a scapegoat.

While Brandy adjusted reasonably well to her foster home, challenges arose. The foster parents, although professing love, set high expectations yet lacked consistency and patience in their interactions. They rarely included Brandy in family activities, expressed annoyance at her demands, and were financially strained. They inconsistently expressed commitment to her care, often contemplating long-term foster care agreements but wavering due to financial concerns. The foster mother struggled with confidentiality, sharing sensitive information, and failed to prioritize essential purchases for Brandy, relying on the social worker for such needs. Brandy's holiday experiences were affected too. She received minimal gifts and was told she hadn't been good enough for Christmas presents. This was likely due to financial constraints and disinterest.

Additionally, community complaints arose, suggesting the foster mother's dissatisfaction with long-term foster care responsibilities impacting her routine. Despite their initial declaration, the foster parents' actions revealed a lack of genuine commitment to Brandy's well-being.

During this period, Brandy underwent physical and mental examinations and started regular counseling. The medical doctor confirmed she had no physical or thyroid issues and that her weight wasn't a concern, as she was likely to slim down with age. Psychiatric evaluation revealed Brandy was not psychotic; her eating issues stemmed from past rejection and poor nurturing in infancy and early childhood. Despite feeling unloved, Brandy developed a positive relationship with her counselor, who believed she could handle upcoming challenges.

However, Brandy's behavior deteriorated; she had temper tantrums and fits, partly exacerbated by counseling. The foster parents struggled to discipline consistently and expressed a desire to have Brandy removed from their home, indicating reluctance to engage in counseling and provide further medical treatment. They even considered rehoming Brandy if their financial situation improved.

Visits with Brandy's mother were scheduled, although the mother resisted reunification efforts. She avoided interactions during visits, often canceling them. Brandy, longing for her mother's love, repeatedly expressed her willingness to change, but her mother dismissively rejected her, eventually demanding an end to all visits and calls, showing no interest in reunification.

Approaching the two-year mark, Brandy's mother chose to surrender her parental rights. She expressed her wish for Brandy to stay in foster care permanently and declined any future visits with her daughter. Brandy's mother was informed that this decision would release Brandy for adoption and the case would transfer to an adoption specialist. Surrender proceedings commenced, and the biological father was approached as a potential caregiver. However, he showed complete disinterest in the child, voluntarily surrendering his rights and stating that neither he nor any of his family members could care for Brandy. The case was transferred to an adoption specialist with the goal being to find a suitable home for Brandy.

⊨⊣⊹⊩⊨

With each page turned, it was as though I was transported back in time, unlocking forgotten chambers of my past. As I sifted through the notes in my Memory Box, my heart started racing just as it had that first day—the day I clenched my small bag of belongings inside a car pulling up to an unfamiliar home. That moment served as a stark reminder of the turbulence that lay ahead.

I refused to step out of the car and demanded to be taken back to my mother, the only anchor in this sea of uncertainty. I ignored the social worker's reassurances and promises I'd see my mother soon as they gently coaxed me out of the vehicle. When I finally stepped through the front door, I was greeted by a couple who claimed to have been waiting for me. The woman's attempted comfort only intensified my sense of disorientation as I was led into the unfamiliar surroundings of this new home. The small, dark, and messy interior stood in stark contrast to the home I had grown accustomed to, leaving me feeling even more out of place. As tears welled up in my eyes, the social worker knelt down to offer comfort, promising that my foster parents would take good care of me. These words felt hollow, as I ached and longed for the familiarity of my old life. I begged to be taken back; I promised to behave if only I could return home. But, as the social worker departed and I was left behind in this strange new place, the reality of the event sunk in. Trapped in a world that felt alien and bleak, I couldn't help but wonder if I would ever find my way back to my mother.

My first night in the unfamiliar foster home was filled with fear and sadness. I lay wide awake in the darkness, the unfamiliar sounds of the house only intensifying my anxiety. Desperate to return home, I drifted into fitful sleep, only to awaken to the same unfamiliar surroundings the next morning. My foster mother's gentle presence offered a glimmer of relief amidst the uncertainty, though my hesitance to let her get close to me spoke volumes about the depth of my longing for home. Through tears, I shared the yearning to return to my mother, clinging to the hope that this nightmare would soon come to an end. In the days that followed, I struggled to connect with this new home and new caregivers, resisting their attempts at warmth and kindness. While the foster father's gestures of affection made me feel uneasy, the foster mother's compassion and understanding offered a small measure of comfort. As I navigated the complexities of this situation, I wondered if this place would ever truly feel like home.

As time wore on, the initial warmth and kindness of the foster parents faded, replaced by a palpable tension and neglect. My foster father withdrew into himself, avoiding interaction with my foster mother, while her appearance and demeanor deteriorated, reflecting a lack of care for herself and for me. The home became more cluttered and unkept, mirroring the disarray within. My foster mother's behavior shifted from compassionate to demanding, her voice raised in frustration as she imposed strict rules and scolded me for minor infractions. They became intimidating and unapproachable, leaving little room for reassurance. Despite a few specific memories of happiness, the environment was charged with uncertainty and fear, lacking the nurturing and support I had desperately craved. I walked on eggshells once again. It became the norm and added to the unease of my new reality. It was a stark reminder that even in a place meant to provide a sanctuary, safety and security was far from guaranteed.

The regular visits with my biological mother, though anticipated with hope, often ended in disappointment and hurt. Despite my efforts to express love and affection, her dismissive and critical remarks ("Why do they dress you in these hideous outfits?" "Your hair is a mess, do they even comb it?") left me feeling unloved and unwanted. The longing to be with her clashed with the harsh reality of her indifference, causing confusion and a deep sadness. Each visit was a painful reminder of the disconnect between my desire for maternal love and her inability to provide it. Enduring her neglect and rejection tested my resilience and left me yearning for a bond that seemed forever out of reach. Despite the hurt, I continued to hold onto the hope that one day she would choose me.

I returned to school as a foster child and repeated first grade. It was both confusing and daunting, yet the familiar setting provided a sense of comfort—it was my safe space. The school, with its well-known hallways and classrooms, had become a refuge among the chaos of my life. As I nervously walked through the entrance, familiar faces greeted me warmly and offered a semblance of normalcy and reassurance. Despite the uncertainty surrounding my personal life, the school remained a constant, a place where I found stability and a touch of kindness.

Recess was a cherished time for me, where I found simple joy playing alone on the monkey bars or admiring patches of flowers along the fence line. I was captivated by their cotton-like heads on long, skinny stems. When my fingers brushed along the stems, the feathery tops would scatter into the air. It became a sport to keep the head intact as I plucked them out of the ground to create the perfect bouquet to offer up as a gift.

My teacher's appreciation of the bundle sparked a meaningful connection. Touched by my gesture, she leaned in with a smile, saying, "Thank you, Brandy. These dandelions are lovely."

Dandelions, I thought to myself, *that's what they are.*

"Did you know dandelions are resilient and magical?" she asked, explaining that although they may seem ordinary and are often considered weeds, they can grow anywhere and in any condition. She told me that the magical part was making a wish while blowing on them, scattering the seeds far and wide. Learning about the magic of dandelions and their ability to carry wishes and dreams resonated deeply with me.

"Would you like to make a wish from this bouquet?" she asked.

My eyes lit up. "Yes, ma'am," I replied eagerly. From that day forward, dandelions became more than just flowers I picked—they became my secret wish-makers, symbols of strength and hope whenever things got tough.

⇥ Seeds of Resilience ⇤

I am inviting you to step into my shoes and experience the world as a declared foster child. As we rifle through this story of a child thrust into a world of uncertainty, consider the remarkable ability I had to adapt and bloom. In the face of a shifting world, full of unfamiliar faces and disappointments, my spirit remained unchanged. I remember desperately wanting an adult to love me, guide me, and make me feel safe. I urge you to consider the profound impact of a parent's choice to forge a life separate from their child. How do you think a child comprehends the concept of a parent choosing a life without them? What hardships might swirl within their young heart? How does a child cope with the innate need for parental love when it is absent? How does this internal conflict shape their sense of self and worth?

As we continue on this journey, let's not merely acknowledge resilience but embrace it as our guiding light, what illuminates the path toward hope and healing. Resilience is more than a trait; it's a force within us, empowering us to rise above setbacks and adapt to adversity, leading to overall mental and emotional well-being.

Resilience is not innate; you're not born resilient. It is an attitude and trait nurtured through experiences and strengthened throughout life. Even if resilience doesn't come naturally, it can be acquired over time—it can be embraced, learned, and honed.

I found resilience through my frustrations with a child protection agency that, despite its mission to safeguard children's well-being, subjected me to my mother's ongoing rejection. While I acknowledge the system's primary aim of family reunification, I question the necessity of exposing my vulnerable spirit to two years of my mother's animosity. It seems somewhat excessive, particularly when my mother explicitly expressed uncertainty about her love for me and blamed me for her marital issues.

Eventually, throughout my experiences, I found comfort in the belief that everything happens for a reason, and realized my pursuit for the truths within my own experience ultimately led to a deeper sense of identity. I can try to understand the reasons people had for their behavior in the past, and use that understanding to see more clearly the struggles of others. It won't always excuse past actions, or detract from my feelings, but it all helps me to understand that the actions of others are never a reflection of my worth.

Embracing this truth freed me from the burden of trying to change something beyond my control. It helped me find a sense of purpose and unintentionally granted me the space I needed to be okay with some hard truths. This courage empowered me to pour my innermost sentiments onto the pages of this memoir, letting them flow freely. Embracing this reality and delving into these candid reflections allowed me to prioritize my emotional liberation and refocus on nurturing relationships with those who genuinely care about me. I embrace a sense of self-love and acceptance, empowering me to find peace in my inner truth.

Throughout this turbulent childhood chapter of my life, I found refuge. The school staff and assigned social workers became, in the midst of my entry into foster care, the comforting pillars holding me up—their smiles, hugs, and words were beacons of reassurance that I was worthy of care and kindness. There are numerous photos in my Life Book featuring the school personnel, presumably taken on my last day at the school, which serve as a testament to their affection toward me. My social workers were quiet and humble souls. They listened, not just to my words, but to the unspoken fears that haunted me. Their empathy and compassion led me to believe I was not alone.

Reflecting on the cards from my Memory Box penned by these different social workers, I felt a deep sense of reassurance. It was striking to realize that, even as a young child, I left a lasting impression, and they saw something special in me worthy of recalling many years later.

"Brandy, your achievements fill me with immense pride. Despite facing challenging and painful moments, your courage and integrity have propelled you toward success. My respect for you has only deepened since you came into my life as a sweet and adorable child."

"Dear Brandy, I recently had the pleasure of meeting someone significant in your life. She shared pictures of a wonderful and vibrant individual—you! Your spirit has always been truly fantastic. While you've grown from the child I once knew, you continue to hold a special place in my thoughts. Despite the challenges life has thrown your way, don't let them hinder your journey. Brandy, remember, you are a winner!"

Throughout my childhood, these angels embodied hope during a time when hope seemed scarce; they were paving my way to resilience. Their example illustrated the significance of compassion and the transformative power of kindness.

One more card was tucked away in the Memory Box, this one from Val, the social worker assigned to my case when I was 11. She introduced me to Nancy.

> *"Brandy, I'm so very proud of you. Knowing you and watching you grow from a <u>wonderful</u> child into a beautiful, intelligent, & gracious young woman has been one of the delights of my life. I'm so very glad that our lives touched one another's & will always hold you in my heart."*

It served as a poignant reminder of where my resilience brought me. The card represented not just a connection to my liberation from the system that once confined me, but a symbol of the transformative journey that led me toward a brighter and more hopeful future beyond the constraints of the past.

Even as this note and my memories resurfaced, something amazing and unexpected happened. The phone rang and an unknown number flashed on the screen. To my surprise, it was Val on the line. It had been 23 years since our last encounter, yet here she was, reaching out to reconnect. The sheer effort she put into finding my contact information left me speechless—a testament to the depth of her caring nature.

As we spoke, I could feel Val's genuine affection for me in every word she uttered. She told me how often she had thought of me and how dearly she missed me.

Later, she wrote me a deeply touching message:

> *"Brandy you have grown into a strong, forceful, and confident woman. I think over the years you absorbed so many of Nancy's characteristics in your own individual way. She was such a good mom for you as you already had such personal strength and heart when you went to live with her. She always allowed and encouraged you to flourish, enabling the best of you to shine."*

Every word still immediately ignites a renewed sense of purpose as I continue to navigate the road to understanding and healing. It's a powerful reminder that connections matter, and that staying resilient in order to have these connections is important, especially for vulnerable people (children and adults alike) in need of reassurance.

When we acknowledge our resilience, we are realizing our own extraordinary power. It is a testament to our inner strength, reminding us that we've conquered the storms before and can do it again. We're reinforcing our capacity to heal and move forward. Acknowledging resilience can grant us control to shape our narratives, heal our wounds, and move forward with newfound confidence. Building resilience involves developing coping mechanisms and strategies to navigate challenges and bounce back from setbacks. By embracing resilience, we don't just survive—we thrive, drawing from strength to overcome, heal, and triumph.

Reflection

Take a moment to delve into your own story. Reflect on moments where you faced challenges and found the strength to overcome them. These experiences are the building blocks of your resilience, shaping the person you are today.

What battles have you fought and emerged stronger from? Are there unresolved issues or relationships in your life that require closure or the setting of boundaries to facilitate your healing process? How do you cope with setbacks and obstacles? What strategies have you found helpful? How can you nurture resilience in your everyday life?

To develop resilience, consider these strategies:

Developing a Growth Mindset Keep a journal where you reflect on challenges you've faced and identify lessons learned and opportunities for growth rather than viewing them as insurmountable obstacles.

Creating a Social Support Map Build a visual representation of your support network including friends, family, mentors, or community members who can provide encouragement and assistance during difficult times. Brainstorm ways to strengthen those connections.

Practicing Self-Care Prioritize activities that promote physical, emotional, and mental well-being, such as exercising, meditating, or engaging in hobbies.

Taking the Comfort Zone Challenge Step outside your comfort zone by setting a small, achievable goal that pushes you to try something new or face a fear. Reflect on the experience and what you learned from it.

** Write a letter to yourself showing kindness and understanding, acknowledging your worth, strength, and accomplishments, even in moments of struggle or setback.

Seeking Professional Help If needed, don't hesitate to seek support from mental health professionals who can provide guidance and assistance in developing resilience strategies.

6

A SPECIAL PRESENTATION

My mother and father surrendered me for adoption.

Life Book Entry, April 1983

Case Summary, 1983

During Brandy's adoption journey, she experienced significant changes and challenges. We delved into the complex
disruption of her daily life and routine, her anxieties
about adoption, and her readiness to embrace a new family.

In our search for the right adoptive home, we decided
to feature Brandy in a segment on the local news called
"Tuesday's Child." This was a serious endeavor where we
aimed to find her the best possible family.

The response to the "Tuesday's Child" showcase was
overwhelming, with 45 interested callers. After thor-
ough screenings and interviews, we found a suitable home
for Brandy. We believe this family will provide her with
the support and care she needs, making them an excellent
resource for her future.

⚡

As I reflect on my past, memories of sitting across from my social worker as an eight-year-old come flooding back. I was a ball of nerves as she began to speak about something very important, as if the weight of the world didn't already feel heavy on my small shoulders.

"Brandy, you've been incredibly brave and wonderful. We've thought long and hard about what's best for you, and we've decided that you're now freed for adoption."

A sensation ran through me—uncertainty, fear, but also a spark of hope.

"Does this mean I won't see my mom again?" I asked.

The social worker nodded gently. "I know this is hard. But it means you'll have a new family, a forever family who will love you, take care of you, and be there for you just like a family should."

"Will they like me?" I asked, a different emotion coming into my voice.

"I believe they will adore you. You're a special, lovable girl, and you deserve a wonderful family who sees that in you. We'll work with an adoption specialist to find the perfect home for you."

Shortly afterward, we set out to film a segment for "Tuesday's Child," a feature on the local news that spotlighted children in need of adoption. My social worker and an adoption specialist orchestrated a memorable day, enabling me to showcase my resilient spirit and kind nature. Clad in my finest summer attire—a white and blue jumpsuit—with hair styled in pigtails, I had an exhilarating adventure at the zoo, surrounded by cameramen and enthusiastic social workers.

As we traversed the zoo, my eyes sparkled with excitement, drawn particularly to the zoo officer and his horse that walked past me. With timid curiosity, I approached the horse, feeling a mixture of awe and disbelief at being so close to such a magnificent creature. As the cameras rolled, I gently interacted with the horse, petting the side of its neck and blowing kisses in its face. My genuine wonder was captured for the airing segment.

The day unfolded with a delightful paddleboat river ride through the zoo, filled with laughter and the distant roars of zoo animals echoing in the background. Alongside the excitement, I had an underlying sense of something special permeating the air.

Throughout the day, I poured my heart into interviews, sharing stories about my favorite animals, dreams of becoming part of a family, and passion for drawing, coloring, and writing. Despite the challenges I had faced, my positivity remained unwavering. The intent was that my authenticity would shine on the screen and resonate with potential adoptive families.

During my interview, the anchorman articulated my potential, my spirited nature, and my strength in overcoming obstacles. He portrayed a child in need of a home, not as a victim but as a remarkable individual with a promising future ahead. The story we conveyed had the power to deeply resonate with others, instilling a sense of hope and possibility.

Leaving the zoo, I felt restored and valued in a way I hadn't experienced before. It was a glimpse of hope that a loving family was waiting to become a part of my story, ready to embrace me as part of their lives. This newfound positivity and self-assurance remains with me to this day, fueling my belief that a bright future always lays ahead.

⇾ Seeds of Hope ⇽

Embracing hope during trauma, especially for a child like me, can be incredibly tough. The key lies in receiving unconditional love, patience, and understanding. Hope is a vital human emotion that fuels optimism and positive expectations for the future, even in the face of challenges. However, hope does have its limitations; it needs to be balanced with realism to avoid further disappointment. It might not address the root cause of trauma, or provide a magical solution to every problem, but combining hope with practical support, resources, and interventions paves the way for effective coping and healing.

With the guidance of my social worker, I adopted a hopeful attitude, holding onto the idea of finding my forever family. Despite the uncertainty, I was assured that the perfect people were out there for me. Hope became my mindset, helping me to move forward and prepare for a new life with a new family.

Memories of that day—the day I was to embrace the idea of a new family—are etched vividly in my mind, immortalized in the pictures within my Life Book. In each snapshot, the joy and hope that filled my heart are palpable. Hope allowed me to cling to the belief that someone out there would connect with my story on a profound level, and being on TV was my opportunity to share a piece of myself, to connect with a viewer, and inspire them to reach out and invite me into their home. As I left the filming that day, I carried with me the belief that I was worthy of a forever family, and that somewhere out there it was waiting for me.

Reflection

Consider the concept of hope in your healing journey, Reflect on how hope has influenced your mindset and reactions during challenging times. How do you personally define hope? What does it mean to you in the context of your healing journey? How has hope influenced your ability to bounce back from setbacks and challenges? In what ways does hope strengthen your resilience? What practices or activities help you cultivate hope in your daily life? Are there specific activities, people, faith, or rituals that help sustain your sense of hope? Taking time to contemplate these questions can offer valuable insight into your relationship with hope and its role in your healing journey.

To cultivate hope, consider these activities:

Vision Board Create a vision board that visually represents your hopes, dreams, and aspirations. Include images, quotes, and affirmations that inspire and motivate you.

Future Self Letter Write a letter to your future self expressing your hopes and goals for the future. Reflect on what brings you hope and how you plan to work toward those aspirations.

Gratitude Practice Cultivate hope by focusing on the positive aspects of your life through a daily gratitude practice. Write down three things you're grateful for each day, no matter how small.

Goal-Setting Set realistic yet ambitious goals for yourself, breaking them down into manageable steps. Focus on what you can do today to move closer to your desired future.

Community Engagement Get involved in activities or groups that align with your values and bring you a sense of connection and purpose. Whether it's volunteering, joining a club, or participating in community events, engaging with others can foster hope.

Reflection and Affirmation Take time to reflect on the past challenges you've overcome and the strengths you've developed along the way. Affirm your resilience and ability to persevere in the face of adversity, reinforcing a hopeful mindset.

7

BROKEN TIES—THE ADOPTION

I went to the adoptive home. They had two sons. I was very nervous and happy. I did not get along well with the boys. After a while I got used to it. It was all right, but not fair. She let them do a lot of stuff that she wouldn't let me do. After a while we started to have problems in the family. It wasn't my fault. I have rights too. The boys had difficulty learning to have me in the family. I didn't talk to the adoptive mom because she was never nice to me.

The adoption was finalized but it didn't work out.

They were not the right family for me.

Life Book Entry, December 1984

Case Summary, 1984

In the process, a blind showing was arranged with the potential adoptive family, allowing Brandy to interact naturally, unaware of their purpose. The parents, impressed by Brandy's personality, agreed to preplacement visits and created a lifebook for her. After reviewing it, Brandy eagerly anticipated meeting her new family.

The preplacement visits went smoothly, and Brandy grew attached to the family, which consisted of a mother, father, and two natural sons. The parents, who met in the military, shared a deep commitment to family values. They had a remarkable ability to treat each child as an individual with separate needs and desires. They wanted to adopt because they were unable to expand their family through natural means. They felt there were plenty of children not as fortunate as theirs and would like to offer love and happiness. Their aim was to adopt a girl aged three to nine. Their hope was to provide a nurturing environment where the child feels wholly accepted and loved by the entire family.

The family was active, faith-oriented, and loving, providing a stable environment. After Brandy's placement, not only did she demonstrate emotional growth but she also excelled academically. She aimed to please her new parents, displaying good behavior and a positive attitude. Over time, her self-esteem improved, and she felt more secure in her permanent placement.

However, a few months after the adoption, behavioral issues arose. With guidance and support, the parents implemented behavior modification techniques. Brandy, though struggling with past rejection, found assurance in her adoptive family's commitment. Despite some progress, challenges persisted, ultimately leading to a therapy referral.

Tragically, after living in the home for a year and a half, Brandy confided in her mother about the past sexual abuse, which caused her immense distress and fear.

Initially ashamed and fearing rejection, Brandy had hesitated to share her ordeal. The adoptive family, faced with this revelation, decided to surrender Brandy weeks later, marking a heartbreaking turn in her journey.

W hen I recount the experience of my first adoption, I can't help but contrast the vastly differing atmospheres between my past life with my birth family and the life I was introduced to with my adoptive family. As I stepped into the home, every corner resonated with warmth and safety. My new place was spacious and inviting, filled with nice things, and my new parents were kind and caring, doing their best to make me feel loved and cherished. Often they'd tell me, "We chose you, so you're our special little girl." As I settled into my new life, I felt a sense of belonging.

My adoptive father, with his firm yet gentle demeanor, quickly became the pillar of discipline in the household. His humor and fairness wove stability into our daily lives. Meanwhile, my adoptive mother's organized and no-nonsense approach ensured everything ran smoothly, from our schedules to our chores. She took me under her wing, sparing no expense. My bedroom was adorned with pink-and-white decor, and a wardrobe full of new clothes. She took me to the salon for a new haircut and enrolled me in a Weight Watchers program. She emphasized that I was her "special princess" and with that I needed to take care of my body so I could shine brightly, just like a princess should.

Despite the typical sibling rivalry among my new siblings and me, we generally tolerated each other. Sometimes, whenever I wanted to join in their activities and embrace a more tomboyish lifestyle, a touch of competitiveness snuck in, making things a tad messy. Despite that, we relished the freedom of playing outdoors on the expansive property.

My first Christmas with my new family proved to be a truly magical experience, filled with decorating, festive activities, and the joy of waking up to find gifts gathered beneath the lit tree. Among the presents, my very own bike took center stage, positioned perfectly in front of the fireplace, marking the day as unforgettable. The highlight of the new year arrived with our first family vacation to Disney World and the beach. It was a thrilling time, packed with exhilarating rides, encounters with beloved characters, and sandy adventures by the shore.

Upon returning home, I found comfort and joy in the familiar rhythms of church and school life. Within the congregation, I discovered a newfound sense of purpose, eagerly participating in spirited singing and dancing to cherished tunes like "This Little Light of Mine" and "Jesus Loves the Little Children." Each note resonated deeply within me, carrying a message of love and acceptance, reinforcing the importance of embracing my true self and sharing my light with the world. With every sway and verse, I felt a sense of wholeness, as if the music itself was lifting me toward a brighter tomorrow.

My new parents took the initiative to have me baptized within our church. Despite only being acquaintances, they approached a couple within the congregation, asking if they were willing to be my godparents. Deeply honored, the couple was moved by the trust placed in them. After thoughtful consideration, they recognized the opportunity to positively influence a young life.

At the baptism, my godparents wholeheartedly embraced their role, showering me with love and commitment. Their gestures never failed to bring a smile to my face, serving as constant reminders of our special bond.

I felt happy on the surface, but deeper down, I wrestled with an emptiness that seemed to intensify with each passing day. Therapy offered some relief, yet the scars of my past persisted, casting shadows of doubt over my newfound contentment. In a moment of vulnerability, I confided in my adoptive mother, hoping for understanding and reassurance.

I shared my recurring nightmares, haunted memories of my stepfather's actions, and my fear of the dark. I worried about him finding me after I revealed our secret. His threat of harm if I ever told anyone weighed heavily on my heart, casting a shadow over my every thought.

My revelation ignited tensions that fractured the fragile peace of our household. My parents refused to address my past, believing that their love alone should erase my scars. With mounting confusion, my inner light dimmed, and a sudden decision altered everything.

Shortly after my disclosure, I trudged through the door after another long day at school. The sight that greeted me sent chills down my spine. My belongings were scattered around the room. Hastily packed into bags were a few meager possessions. My parents stood nearby, their faces etched with determination, urging me to come with them without explanation. In that moment, a sense of déjà vu washed over me as memories of past upheavals flooded my mind.

Nervousness engulfed me like a suffocating wave, leaving me gasping for air in its wake. With a heavy heart, I realized that, once again, I was being uprooted from that semblance of stability I so craved. My siblings remained behind, their presence a painful reminder of the life I was leaving as I embarked on another journey into the unknown.

As we pulled up to my destination, my eyes fixated on the imposing sign bearing the word "hospital" in bold letters. Stepping inside, I was immediately struck by the vast, sterile environment that surrounded me. The air seemed to hum with an eerie silence, broken only by the distant murmur of hushed voices. At the front desk, my parents exchanged words with the receptionist, their faces etched with urgency. Meanwhile, I stood rooted to the spot, my heart pounding in my chest as I watched the scene unfold before me.

Suddenly, an adult emerged through the oversized hospital doors, and with a gentle but firm hand, guided me away from my parents, leading me down a maze of hallways that seemed to twist and turn endlessly. As we walked, the sterile scent of antiseptic filled my nostrils, mingling with the faint aroma of dread permeating every corner of the hospital. Each step I took felt heavier than the last, as if I was trudging through quicksand. Finally, we arrived at a nondescript room tucked away in a remote corner of the hospital. With a solemn nod, the adult gestured for me to enter, helped me get settled, and left me alone with my thoughts and jitters.

❧ Seeds of Character ❧

As you continue to follow the intricate narrative of my life, I urge you to consider the profound complexity and sensitivity that envelop a child's heart when faced with the bewildering reality that they are not wanted, grappling with confusion and hurt all the while, longing for stability. Trust is fragile and the quest for acceptance is both desperate and profound. I encourage you to consider the impact your empathy and understanding can have on the lives of children facing similar struggles. Imagine the child's questions about their worthiness—Am I unlovable? Did I do something wrong?

As I look back on my experience, I learned a valuable lesson that would shape my view of the world and my place in it. I discovered the world can be cruel. Having hope repeatedly shattered and trust easily broken led me to be cautious, guarding my heart from betrayal. I meticulously crafted a shield to protect myself from past scars and the possibility of getting new ones. Molded by diverse factors like upbringing, experiences, culture, and personal choices, sad moments and hard struggles were profoundly influencing how I interacted with the world and others.

My sensitivity, stemming from feeling unloved and unworthy, was profoundly impacting my personality. It had begun with my biological mother openly expressing her disgust toward me, repeatedly denying me affection. I struggled with low self-esteem, which took a toll on my confidence and social interactions. Convinced that I was undeserving of love, I withdrew from connections, leading to a profound sense of loneliness. I became a people pleaser, neglecting my own needs in pursuit of approval. Fearing rejection, I avoided forming emotional bonds as a shield against potential hurt, manifesting most noticeably in my lack of trust. My character and emotional temperament were at risk, along with my self-worth.

As I gaze at my childhood photos stored in the Memory Box, it's incomprehensible to me how anyone could speak so negatively about a child; how their poor character could so easily put my own at risk. These pictures, taken during my time with my biological mother, depict a truly precious little girl—despite what my mother claimed.

Growing up, I faced repeated rejection, making it difficult for me to trust and impacting my perspective on love and connection in future relationships. Even today, I shy away from affection and affirmations, maintaining a personal perimeter. If someone inches too close, I become uncomfortable. My closest inner circle would agree it's hard for me to offer physical warmth. I have a completely different love language!

Acknowledging that these feelings of doubt were products of my past trauma was crucial. Although certain traits occasionally resurface, I've cultivated coping mechanisms to maintain my strong character. Through resilience, embracing my positive qualities, and relying on my support system, I actively strive to construct a hold onto a positive and empowered self-image, triumphing over the challenges that once harmed my character.

During my lifelong healing process, I am making small strides to step out of my comfort zone, starting with embracing hugs—not just receiving but initiating them. The more I expose myself to this act, the more relaxed I become. It's surprising at my age to realize the power of a hug!

This process of healing has also led me to educate myself and led to some insightful discoveries. I turned to literature for insight, and to my surprise, I stumbled upon quite a bit of information about toxic family dynamics. In a way it's comforting to know I'm not the only one navigating these complexities.

According to Peg Streep's article "How Toxic Families Choose a Child to Scapegoat" in *Psychology Today*, toxic families often choose a scapegoat to maintain the illusion of a healthy family dynamic. Streep explains that "Scapegoating permits a parent to think of the family as healthier and more functioning than it actually is; if it weren't for that one individual—yes, the scapegoat—the family would be perfect, and life would be blissful." Streep identifies various roles that members of a family take on, such as The Resistor, The Sensitive One, or The Outlier. I realize I was The Reminder, the child who supposedly resembles someone who is disliked and even hated. I faced an impossible dilemma growing up—my mother openly admitted that her hateful feelings toward my father affected her love for me, and my stepfather didn't want to raise another man's child. I now understand that there was nothing I could have done to improve those relationships.

Next I encountered my prospective adoptive parents, who were committing to a nine-year-old in foster care. Despite my baggage, they made me a member of their family. But instead of embracing my vulnerabilities, my adoptive parents dismissed my pain, urging me to bury my past. I became a canvas on which they painted their ideal image, coached to be someone I was not and forced to fulfill someone else's desires. They drowned out my cries for help and healing, forming character traits that pushed things away instead of confronting them to create my true identity.

Ironically, my new parents and I shared a common desire to leave the past behind, but our approaches differed significantly and my character took another hit. I was learning that to truly be wanted and valued I had to leave the life I knew, the person I was, in the rear view mirror.

Today I can't help but speculate about my first adoptive parents' true intentions. I suspect my adoptive mother was in it for herself—a "look what we did" type of person. It felt like her desire to rescue me was more about gaining recognition and praise than genuinely caring about my needs.

Recently, I came across an article by Dr. Stephan Poulter, a family therapist, titled "The Five Mother Types." As I consider the adoptive mother-daughter relationship I had, two of Poulter's mother types stand out to me: the Perfectionist Mother, who is overly controlling and values appearance above all, and the Me-First Mother, who is self-absorbed and views her children as tools to make herself shine. Seeing my adoptive mother through this lens helps me, again, to understand it was her, not me, and gives me space to continue refining my character. This introspective process reveals subtle nuances and insights that were previously hidden from my understanding.

Four decades later, as I reflect, I wonder: If I had erased my memories and forgotten my biological mother and everything I was exposed to, could I have led a seemingly normal life? Such compliance might have spared me the subsequent chapters of my story, preventing the need for this narrative. However, the reality is that I was merely 10 years old—far from emotionally mature enough to comprehend and meaningfully contribute to my own healing. Ignoring the past would have left an open wound inside of me that would have simply festered. It would have done more damage over time to my character. It would have ultimately held me back.

It seems my adoptive mother, believing I was irreparably damaged, opted to take drastic measures and abandon the adoption ship. All of this contributed to who I became and is now something I look back on to try and better myself.

My perfectionist nature likely originated from these formative years because of the environment I found myself in. It has been a personal challenge for me to move away from my classic Type A personality, but each day I make a conscious effort to give myself grace for at least one thing. Even if I'm only 5 minutes late instead of 15 minutes early!

I also battle against a natural need for self-preservation—for leaving things in the past, which also stemmed from this time. While these instincts were bittersweet, they sharpened my understanding of the world and honed my approach to navigate its challenges. Today it's astonishing to me how irrational it is to carry the weight of the past by ignoring it, so I work to evolve and conquer adversity. Through my experiences of enduring others' broken commitments, my new, spring-into-action strategy makes it possible for me to now cope with arduous circumstances.

Looking deep into who I am today, I realize that I am a "doer." I may not be very good with words or verbal expression, and I'm okay with that because words are nothing without action. My actions speak volumes. When I am passionate and committed to something, I put my all into it, showcasing my character through my efforts. This book is a prime example of my actions. Despite all the ups and downs and moments when I wanted to give up, I pushed on because I made a commitment to myself and the healing process. And, yes, I probably overdo it sometimes. Like that night I stayed up organizing my thoughts into Venn diagrams, arranging colored sticky notes in perfect chronological order, and declaring the dining room walls as my command center for the book—all because I didn't want to miss a single detail. But if you're going to do something, you might as well do it with gusto!

Reflection

In contemplating the development of your character, ponder these questions: How have the experiences you've endured shaped the person you are today? I invite you to consider moments in your life when you've faced significant challenges. How did your mind and body respond? What coping mechanisms did you develop, and how did they shape your perspective and resilience? Can you identify instances where adversity led to personal growth and transformation? How can understanding your survival instinct empower you to navigate future challenges with greater resilience?

Consider in your reflection if you have any negative beliefs or self-talk patterns that hinder your progress, and how you can challenge or change them. What activities or hobbies bring you joy and fulfillment, and how can you incorporate them more into your life to enhance your overall well-being?

To explore the concept of character, consider these activities:

Values Assessment Reflect on your core values and beliefs. Identify what matters most to you and how these values shape your actions and decisions.

Character Strengths Inventory Take a character strengths assessment or survey, readily available online. Reflect on your top strengths and how you can leverage them in your daily life.

Character Sketch Create a detailed character sketch for a fictional character, highlighting their personality traits, motivations, and moral compass. Then create one for yourself.

Ethical Dilemma Discussion Engage in a group discussion or debate about ethical dilemmas and moral decision-making. Explore different perspectives and consider how character influences choices.

Role Model Reflection Identify a role model or mentor who embodies the qualities you admire. Reflect on their character traits and the impact they have had on your own development.

Service Learning Project Get involved in a service learning project that allows you to apply your character strengths and values while making a positive contribution to your community. Reflect on how the experience has shaped your character and worldview.

8

BEHIND CLOSED DOORS

They took me to a hospital. That felt horrible!
They didn't even tell me! They lied to me!
I'm mad at them because they didn't tell me.

Life Book Entry, January 1985

Case Summary, 1985

Shortly before arriving at the state hospital, Brandy underwent a psychological evaluation. The psychologist observed that Brandy had developed deep-seated beliefs about herself as being ugly, worthless, and unlovable. The traumatic experience of sexual abuse intensified these negative feelings. Brandy's distress was so overwhelming that minor punishments felt like complete rejection, triggering panic attacks and leading her to lie to avoid rejection. Her primary fear was being given up by her adoptive parents, causing her to withdraw, exhibit anger, and become noncommunicative. She was diagnosed with Severe Adjustment Disorder with Mixed Disturbance of Emotions and Conduct, along with severe depression. Intense psychotherapy and short-term hospitalization were recommended to help her address the pain from her past and modify her behaviors.

A week later, a psychiatric evaluation diagnosed Brandy with Dysthymic Disorder-severe and Atypical Personality Disorder, leading to the recommendation for hospitalization. Four days after the evaluation, Brandy was placed in the state hospital. Choosing not to deal with the issues, the adoptive parents surrendered her to state custody. After a few weeks in the hospital, Brandy's adoptive mother visited her once to inform her that they had surrendered her to state custody and would no longer keep in touch. They also refused to return her belongings, claiming they had been destroyed during Brandy's outbursts.

Brandy stayed in the state facility for six months, showing good progress with no signs of depression during her hospitalization. The final diagnosis was Dysthymic Disorder with a positive prognosis, as long as she did not face another episode of rejection. It was recommended that Brandy receive individual therapy on a weekly basis to address symptoms such as withdrawal, sleep disturbances, crying, hiding food, resistance to bathing, and lying to avoid taking responsibility for her inappropriate behaviors.

As I reflect on my past, memories of a tender age emerge. My sense of abandonment within the confines of the hospital resonated deeply, evoking memories of feeling lost and alone in unfamiliar surroundings. It was a place meant for healing, yet it felt like a desolate sanctuary for lost souls, where the forgotten or ignored found refuge in the shadows.

The day I was abandoned at the hospital remains etched in my memory like a haunting nightmare. As my adoptive parents walked away, I felt myself disappearing behind the heavy doors, thrust into a world where reality and illusions blurred.

Within the hospital walls, my days were regimented by routines that offered a semblance of structure amongst the chaos of my sorrow. Though the staff attempted to provide comfort to us children, their efforts felt distant and inadequate. In the solitude of my small room, I encountered unanswerable questions, while loneliness became my constant companion. The sterile white walls served as stark reminders of shattered hopes and dreams, amplifying the ache in my heart.

I often found myself subjected to the constant intrusion of medical instruments and probing questions, with little regard for personal boundaries or genuine conversation. While the staff had well-meaning intentions, their empathy was often overshadowed by detachment. They moved about the ward, administering medication and checking on rooms, their presence affirming my lack of control.

Therapy sessions were agonizing, as therapists dissected my thoughts and moods, leaving me feeling exposed and vulnerable. I often felt talked at rather than listened to, as they dominated the conversation with their insights and advice.

They threw out terms I couldn't possibly understand. They slapped more labels on me than a discount store during a clearance sale! I was diagnosed with Severe Adjustment Disorder with Mixed Disturbance of Emotions and Conduct, severe depression or Dysthymic Disorder—severe and Atypical Personality Disorder. I mean, were they trying to fill up my medical record like a shopping cart on Black Friday?

In simpler terms, Adjustment Disorder with Mixed Disturbance of Emotions and Conduct, as defined by Collective Social Services, involves an exaggerated response to a stressful life event, leading to negative behavioral changes and emotional instability. Symptoms may include distress, significant behavioral impact, loss of interest in enjoyable activities, feelings of sadness or depression, anxiety, panic attacks, and behavioral issues. According to the Mayo Clinic, many individuals with adjustment disorders benefit from brief treatment, while others with persistent issues may require longer intervention.

Dysthymia, a type of chronic depression, lacks a clear cause, though chronic stress and trauma have been associated with its development. Symptoms include a persistent sad or empty mood, reduced ability to concentrate, low energy, fatigue, feelings of hopelessness, changes in weight and appetite, altered sleep patterns, and low self-esteem. To diagnose dysthymia in children and adolescents, a depressed mood must persist for at least one year, accompanied by at least two of the mentioned symptoms. In the American Psychiatric Association's Diagnostic and Statistical Manual of Mental Disorders, fourth edition, text revision (DSM-IV-TR), there's a category of personality disorders for which there is insufficient evidence for a more specific designation, indicating the presence of a disorder without meeting the criteria for a particular personality disorder.

Attending school in the hospital setting presented unique challenges. The antiseptic environment did not replicate a normal school atmosphere, and while classes provided structure, I struggled to form meaningful connections with my peers. Instead, I withdrew and shut down internally, disconnecting from my surroundings as a means of coping. In my isolation, I felt muted, numb, and invisible.

I remember contracting mononucleosis during my hospital stay, a viral infection known for causing severe fatigue, sore throat, and fever. Due to its contagious nature, I was isolated from other patients and staff, confined to a small room with minimal amenities. The hospital staff took extensive precautions, dressing in protective gear whenever they entered my room. The sight of them in masks and gloves only added to my anxiety.

The illness left me unable to eat and extremely fatigued. I required assistance with even basic tasks. The prolonged duration of the virus took a toll on me emotionally too, compounding the challenges I was already facing in the hospital. It was a difficult time, further exacerbating my sense of vulnerability and isolation.

During my time in seclusion, I often found myself staring at the blank walls, reminiscing about the bouquet of dandelions I once gave to my teacher. I remembered blowing on them with all my might, hoping that my wish for a family would come true. But, as with many things in my life, it seemed that my hopes had been shattered once again. Why was I left behind? What had I done wrong? Was this place to be my new forever home? The uncertainty and lack of communication about my situation only added to my anxiety. Contemplating growing up in such a place was a lonely and daunting prospect. I even lashed out while alone in my room, yelling into the air and taking my feelings out on my pillow. I felt as if the dandelion had abandoned me after I had sent out my wish far and wide for a family.

⇥ Seeds of Forgiveness ⇤

Imagine standing before a door, full of vulnerability, hoping for acceptance. Then the door closes with a resounding thud. Rejection is not just a word, it's a sharp, searing sensation that pierces. It's the feeling of being deemed unworthy, undesirable, or unlovable. Every rejection is a heavy stone I add to the backpack of my self-worth, a reminder there is something wrong with me.

This is how I felt during my hospital stay, and it took me a significant part of a month to navigate through the pain. Between the highs and lows of my childhood, this particular episode stirs up immense bitterness and resentment within me. Confronting the vulnerability of being abandoned not once, but twice, is an excruciating task. I held onto the hope for a family that would wholeheartedly accept me, craving understanding rather than pity. I longed for others to acknowledge that my struggle was not a choice but a profound emotional battle. I begged for someone to reach out and say, "I see you, you are not alone." The ache to express my feelings clashed with the fear of judgment and rejection, trapping me in a constant inner struggle. I felt like I wasn't enough, that I fell short of expectations, and that I didn't deserve love. I questioned what I could have done differently to avoid this rejection. Holding onto hope and trusting others' intentions, words, or affections became an uphill challenge.

One day, while writing this book, the weight of these events carried so much baggage for me that I ended up setting my keyboard aside and simply letting the tears flow—giving in to a good, old-fashioned cry and temper tantrum. I confronted the harsh truth that I, as a child, held no inherent worth. This revelation weighed heavily on me, leaving me sprawled on the couch, questioning my decision once again to embark on this emotional journey. The haunting question "Why was I not enough?" consumed my thoughts. In the days that followed, I faced the idea that I could never empathize with my adoptive parents. They knowingly welcomed a broken child from foster care into their home, promising unconditional love, only to deem me irreparable when my scars surfaced.

Out of 45 prospective families, I couldn't help but wonder: Was this truly the cream of the crop? I mean, were the other 44 families just in it for the free coffee at the adoption agency during screenings? I laugh at this and move on, my soul ready to push forward.

Looking back, it's evident that my vulnerability and actions aligned with the criteria for my diagnosis. But if someone had just taken the time to invest in me, I could have learned some valuable coping skills instead of feeling like I was constantly hitting rock bottom. Just a little support and guidance, whether I could have asked for it or not, could have changed the whole game for me.

I know I must find a way to let go of the feelings associated with my adoptive parents. These unresolved emotions have the potential to negatively affect my peace if left unchecked. By attempting to empathize, I can start to unravel the complex emotions that bind me to this pain and move forward with a clearer heart and mind.

Developing empathy requires me to consider their fears, insecurities, and perhaps even their misguided attempts to handle a difficult situation. After my disclosure to them, they might have feared I would turn on them and make accusations, potentially diminishing their reputation or status. This might have driven their actions, though it doesn't excuse the hurt they caused.

As I struggle to see things from their perspective, this is all I can muster for now. With this limited progress, I contemplate if there is another avenue to freeing myself from this past pain. It might seem daunting, but exploring different paths could be the key to liberation and opening the door to an unburdened future.

Going through this process was never about forgiveness for me. I'd been told countless times that forgiveness is crucial, but I'd resisted, feeling no one had acknowledged their wrongdoing. So why do I owe them this?

Today feels different, possibly because I've embraced vulnerability. Forgiveness may seem like a distant goal, but it also may be the key to freeing myself from this pain.

I'm reminded of a particular Sunday message given by Kendrick Vinar at Grace Church in Chapel Hill, North Carolina, that deeply resonated with me. He spoke of casting our burdens on the Lord and trusting in a just judge to sort things out.

It's common to hold onto anger when we've been hurt, wronged, or abused. However, clinging to anger only perpetuates harm within ourselves. Ironically, by refusing to forgive, we allow the person who hurt us to continue hurting us. Forgiveness takes faith, trusting that justice will be served by a higher power. The message was clear: trust God in the process, learn to let go, and ask for blessings for that individual.

As Martin Luther King once said, "Darkness cannot drive out darkness; only light can do that. Hate cannot drive out hate; only love can do that." It takes strength to forgive, to move in the opposite spirit with humility. Inspired by the message, I am committed to praying for those from my past, to genuinely wish them well, and to move toward forgiveness. I choose to trust in a just judge and let go of my anger and disdain for them.

I found forgiveness manifesting through prayer. My first prayer was for my biological father, as he was the most recent presence in my life. It was brief, yet purposeful. "God, I struggle to forgive others—I'm sorry. You always give me grace when I mess up, and I want to extend that same grace to my dad. Bless him and help me to let go. Amen." I've resolved to continue this practice, working through the list of individuals I harbor hard feelings toward, forgiving myself for what I've held onto and forgiving them for what I can. I've come to understand that it's not about condoning or forgetting what happened, but about releasing the emotional burden that comes with holding grudges.

Forgiveness and establishing healthy boundaries go hand-in-hand in the journey toward healing. Forgiveness frees us from resentment, while setting boundaries empowers us to protect our well-being by saying no to things that don't align with our values or that make us uncomfortable. Together, they form a foundation for self-respect and empowerment, leading to greater emotional resilience and overall well-being.

With each act of forgiveness, I find strength. Although I've forgiven my biological father, I've also set conscientious boundaries to protect myself from disappointment and heartache. This might eventually lead me to let go of the unrealistic relationship altogether. As I move through the despair, I remind myself to embrace the inherent messiness of life, consciously seeking the silver lining in every experience.

Forgiveness has allowed me to reclaim my power and move forward without being weighed down by past hurts. It's a process that takes a considerable amount of time but it leads me to a sense of inner peace and freedom.

Reflection

Reflecting on the following questions can provide valuable insights into your own beliefs and feelings about forgiveness. What does forgiveness mean to you personally? Do you believe forgiveness is a choice or a gradual process? Are there specific events or people in your life that you find it difficult to forgive? Why? How does holding onto grudges or refusing to forgive affect your emotional well-being? In your opinion, does forgiveness require reconciliation with the person who hurt you, or is it a personal journey, independent of the other party?

It's also worthwhile at this point to consider the role of self-worth and self-respect in establishing healthy boundaries. How does valuing yourself influence your ability to set and maintain boundaries? Reflect on any patterns or recurring themes in your relationships that may indicate a need for boundary setting. What steps can you take to address these patterns? Reflect on a time when setting boundaries resulted in a positive outcome or improved your well-being. What lessons did you learn from that experience?

To explore forgiveness, try these activities:

Letter Writing Exercise Write a letter to someone who has wronged you, expressing your feelings and thoughts about the situation. Practice forgiveness by letting go of resentment and offering understanding or compassion.

Reflection Journal Keep a forgiveness journal, where you reflect on past hurts and your journey toward forgiveness. Write about the challenges, insights, and healing that come with forgiving others and yourself.

Role Reversal Put yourself in the shoes of the person you need to forgive. Consider their perspective, their motivations, and the experiences that may have led to their actions. This exercise can foster empathy and aid in the forgiveness process.

Guided Meditation Engage in forgiveness-focused meditation practices that help you release negative emotions and cultivate feelings of acceptance and peace toward yourself and others.

Group Discussion Participate in a group discussion or support group focused on forgiveness. Share your experiences, challenges, and insights with others who are also on a journey toward forgiveness.

Random Acts of Kindness Practice forgiveness by performing acts of kindness toward others, even those who have wronged you. This can help shift your focus away from resentment and toward empathy and compassion.

9

BREAKING FREE

But as it turns out I'm glad because I didn't want to live with them and now I live with my godparents.

Life Book Entry, July 1985

Case Summary, 1985

During Brandy's struggles, the adoptive mother confided in the godmother, indicating they were having a lot of trouble with her. Concerned, the godparents offered to provide a respite, keeping Brandy for the weekend. However, the mother declined, opting instead to hospitalize Brandy. The following week the church pastor broke the news to the godparents about Brandy's placement in the state hospital, leaving them devastated.

Attempts to visit Brandy were prohibited by restrictions imposed by the hospital, despite daily calls from the distressed godparents seeking answers. The hospital explained they didn't want Brandy forming new relationships, but the godmother insisted this was an existing, meaningful bond. Denied access, the godparents confronted the adoptive mother, only to be dismissed. Eventually, the parents revealed their decision not to reclaim Brandy.

Outraged, the godparents insisted on a visit to reassure Brandy of their ongoing support. Granted permission, they discovered that the adoption had indeed been dissolved, and Brandy was back in the state's custody.

During this time, Brandy fell ill with mono, halting visitations. Recognizing the legal limbo, the facility collaborated with the godparents. They spoke with the psychologist, finding no evidence justifying Brandy's continued hospitalization. Encouraged to become certified foster parents, the godparents agreed and fulfilled the requirements. Meanwhile, the godfather's new job transferred them to a new city. The week of their move, Brandy was released from the hospital into the godparents' care, and the case was transferred to another state agency, marking the beginning of their journey as foster parents.

＝≼+ +≽＝

U nbeknownst to me, the godparents my adoptive parents had selected during my baptism were deeply committed to their role. I hadn't known they'd stayed committed even after my adoptive family relinquished their rights, but after some time in the hospital, I was suddenly granted visitation and day outings with my godfamily. My adult godsister, conveniently located nearby, became a regular presence in my life. Though memories from this period are hazy due to my emotional shutdown, I distinctly remember experiencing joy in their presence. These moments became a source of warmth and happiness while I was in the hospital.

⇥ Seeds of Gratitude ⇤

Gratitude has become my faithful companion throughout this journey. Perhaps shaped by my past experiences, I've naturally grown into a grateful person and one who counts blessings. Reflecting on how things could have taken a darker turn, I've embraced a "Focus on the Good" perspective in recent years.

Overcoming the tendency to anticipate the worst has been a significant challenge, rooted in years of expecting joyous moments to be swiftly followed by sorrow. However, through diligent effort, I've been working to retrain my mindset, allowing myself to break free from the shackles of negativity and anxiety. Learning to live in the present moment has become my mantra, and has allowed me to create a sanctuary where worries lose their power and calm exists among life's uncertainties.

Gratitude first comes to me as I contemplate that pivotal moment when my biological mother relinquished me to the state's custody. Though her actions were born from selfish motives, the magnitude of her decision dawns upon me like a revelation. If I had stayed in that volatile and abusive environment, I could have faced dire consequences, including the stark possibility of death. Now, with clarity born of hindsight, I realize the profound favor given to me by her relinquishment. I am keenly aware of my fortune to have escaped that unstable situation, and my gratitude knows no bounds.

The journey I've traveled often leads me to ask, "Why me? Why did I survive?" Reflecting on my exit from the foster care system decades ago, I realize how lucky I am to have defied the odds. I am sincerely grateful for the strength I've cultivated and the person I've evolved into through the unwavering support of the people who nurtured me and became my voice throughout my journey—be it the dedicated school staff, social workers, or countless others who played a role in shaping my path. People like Val, who highlighted the power of advocacy and the gratitude that can result when one speaks up. Recently, she brought up the subject of my Life Book, asking if I still had it. I couldn't help but chuckle at her mention of it, amazed that she remembered it after all these years.

As we reminisced about the Life Book, I shared with her how it had evolved into something more profound than just a collection of memories. It had become the foundation for this memoir—a testament to the journey I'd been on and the person I'd become.

Val recounted a story of her own connection with the Life Book that I'd never heard before. When my case was transferred to her, she learned about the existence of my Life Book and was eager to get it in her possession. But to her shock, she discovered that the book had been left with my adoptive parents.

With determination, Val reached out to my adoptive mother to inquire about the whereabouts of the Life Book. What she heard in response was both shocking and heartbreaking. My adoptive mother callously declared, "I burned that M.F." before abruptly hanging up the phone on her.

The callousness of my adoptive mother's actions left Val reeling. "She had no right to do that," Val said. "She dismissed years of your history in an instant." But Val refused to let my story be silenced. She embarked on a mission, pulling together all available contacts and resources to recreate the earlier days documented in the Life Book, ensuring that my journey would continue to be noted and honored.

Val's determination to preserve my story reaffirmed the impact of her unwavering dedication to me, and it's with a great sense of gratitude that I look at it now. It is a poignant reminder of the significance of positive influences in shaping one's journey, even in the face of adversity.

Reflection

Expressing gratitude can be a powerful tool in the healing process. It shifts focus from what's lacking to what's present, fostering a positive mindset and improving mental well-being.

Reflect on moments when expressing gratitude made a difference in your outlook. How has adopting a thankful perspective impacted your well-being? Consider the challenges you've faced—did gratitude play a role in overcoming them? What daily practices can you incorporate to cultivate a more grateful mindset and enhance your healing journey?

To cultivate gratitude, consider these activities:

Keep a Gratitude Journal Write down things you're thankful for daily, reflecting on both big and small blessings.

Express Appreciation Verbally express gratitude to those who have positively impacted your life, whether it's friends, family, or colleagues.

Practice Mindfulness Incorporate mindfulness exercises into your routine, such as meditation or deep breathing, to increase awareness of the present moment and cultivate gratitude.

Count Your Blessings Take time to pause and reflect on the abundance in your life, focusing on what you have rather than what you lack.

Volunteer or Help Others Engage in acts of kindness and service to others, which can enhance feelings of gratitude and fulfillment.

Shift Perspective When facing challenges, try to find silver linings or lessons to be grateful for, reframing negative situations into opportunities for growth.

10

GUIDING LIGHT

It felt good to be with Pa-ran and Na-nan. It made me happy. I was in the 5th grade & I also took violin lessons. I made a lot of friends in school & in the neighborhood. I met all the family—there are lots of aunts, uncles & cousins. I had a party for my birthday, that was fun. And Christmas was nice too.

I would like to stay with them and be adopted. That is what they want to do also.

Sometimes it might get hard to be in a family—but we will all try to work & talk our problems out.

That's what helps to make a family good.

Life Book Entry, January 1986

Case Summary, 1986

Upon leaving the state hospital, Brandy found placement with her godparents who, distressed by the rejection from the adoptive parents, began visiting her regularly. Eventually certified as foster parents, they initially expressed a strong desire to adopt Brandy. However, after the adoption subsidy request was initiated, her disruptive behaviors, including lying, verbal abuse, talking back, and occasional property damage, escalated significantly.

Despite the godparents' certification as an adoptive family, Brandy's acting out prompted rising anxiety about her behaviors and their own capacity to manage them. Although Brandy acknowledges her disruptive actions, she claims indifference, citing a belief that it's unjust. Oddly, she expresses a genuine desire to be adopted by them and wishes for a successful family dynamic.

The godparents, whose grown children have left home, admit to having low tolerance for defiant behavior, particularly children "talking back." Dissatisfied with Brandy's progress in family counseling, they initiated weekly psychotherapy with a psychologist and have requested a halt to the adoption process. Frustration with Brandy's perceived disrespect has led them to contemplate her placement to a group home, with the condition that she must change her behavior to return.

In the sixth grade, Brandy excels academically, receiving regular education with speech therapy. Despite her engaging and likable demeanor, she displays theatrical and demanding traits. Resistance to therapy persists as she strives to move past her troubled past, wanting to "put it all behind her." She continues to encounter confusion over her birth mother's rejection and has concern for her half-sibling's safety. Brandy participated in a six-week group to talk about feelings associated with birth parents, foster care, and adoption. She clearly felt the other children in the group could not relate to her painful experiences and she had the tendency to assert herself by being bossy.

A comprehensive psychological assessment was conducted to guide future plans for her. The analysis of her personality revealed challenges in emotionally stepping back and grasping complete situations. Coping with minor stressors in her environment was noted to be difficult. Mild oppositional tendencies were observed, leading to conflicts with rules and regulations. Brandy tends to internalize anger, resorting to aggressive and verbal expressions when unsuccessful. Her ability to connect with others on a deeper interpersonal level is lowered, indicating difficulties in trusting. The diagnostic impression points to Adjustment Disorder with Atypical Features.

Brandy could benefit from individual psychotherapy to address underlying conflicts, and family supportive therapy would aid in understanding and navigating her problems. It is crucial for anyone working with Brandy to unequivocally accept her as a person without threatening rejection, as her fear of rejection significantly impacts her ability to adjust in different environments. Improving her receptive and expressive vocabulary is essential, and encouragement to ask questions, describe activities, and explore reading in her areas of interest is important. Despite facing challenges due to past deprivation and abuse, Brandy demonstrates good, bright, normal intelligence that can be nurtured with appropriate support.

—⊰†⊱—

I found a faint ray of hope with my godparents. I affectionately referred to them as Pa-ran and Na-nan, the French equivalents of godfather and god-mother. Addressing new parental figures had always been tricky for me, and I often hesitated to associate anyone with the revered titles of mother or father. The names my godparents offered seemed perfect.

Surrounded by an extended family, I found myself immersed in a world of warmth and care, where memorable holiday gatherings become a cherished tra-dition. Birthdays, once downplayed, now blossomed into vibrant celebrations. However, despite the festive atmosphere, my own birthday remained a sensitive topic, tinged with a lingering discomfort about the significance of my existence.

Slowly but surely, I began to adapt to my new environment, mustering the courage to step out of my self-imposed isolation. Shielding myself from forming attachments had become second nature, yet breaking free from this protective shell meant confronting the possibility of self-sabotage, a skill I had mastered. Testing boundaries had become my way of discerning others' commitment to me, although I can't recall specific instances; it was likely a subconscious pattern I had woven into my interactions.

Pa-ran and Na-nan upheld a highly structured and disciplined lifestyle. While Pa-ran's approach was stern, it was always infused with love. Na-nan had a gentler touch. Despite their firmness, I never felt afraid of them, which spoke volumes about their nurturing demeanor.

However, the introduction of counseling in this home environment marked a deviation from our positive trajectory. Historically, such interventions signaled a looming issue, indicating I was veering off course and was in need of a correc-tive action.

❦ Seeds of Understanding ❦

Confronting this particular chapter demands frequent pauses, weighed down by questions such as, Was my mother right? Was I the issue? Was all this pain self-inflicted? While I once prided myself on skillfully pushing such feelings aside and forging ahead, my commitment to personal growth and this ongoing journey now compels me to confront the disturbance rather than merely sidestep it. In my search to understand, I find myself struggling not to internalize the simmering outrage that threatens to consume me. I intentionally carve out moments, sometimes days, to embrace coping mechanisms like devotion, online worship, deep breathing, old-fashioned bawling, and chores—there's something soothing about decluttering and organization! These practices have become essential in guiding me through this challenging period and breaking free from my irrational thoughts.

On a particularly daunting day of writing, I felt tempted to take a mental health day from work. However, I mustered the strength to compartmentalize and push through my routine. A small act of kindness from a colleague helped restore my courage to keep working through my story, prompting me to confront the tough questions surrounding my godparents. Who would have suspected that a simple gift of candy from a colleague who said, "I thought of you when I saw the bag in the store" could spark a renewed sense of worth and purpose? Apparently, dark chocolate has that effect on me!

Despite the portrayal, I know with certainty that my godparents are good people. They found themselves tasked with the responsibility of raising me, forced to make life-altering decisions swiftly amidst confusion. They navigated the complex process largely on their own, facing my significant underlying issues and considerable challenges.

My memories are brimming with happiness and love with this bustling family. Despite the usual testing of boundaries and occasional expressions of anger— admittedly, I was mouthy and could throw a fit worthy of an Oscar—we always managed to see it through. Regular sessions with my new social worker, Val, were part of my routine and a positive connection was formed. However, the sudden disruption of my placement, being taken away from the supportive environment of my godparents' home and sent to the children's home, remains perplexing. There was a lack of communication about the plans for me, and my godparents remained out of sight. According to my social worker, my godparents were getting too old to look after a child like me, emphasizing the need for me to be in a setting that could meet my needs. Despite harboring uncertain feelings about the interference in my relationship with my godparents, I'd concluded that perhaps this separation was meant as a respite for us—providing us space from one another to decompress and regroup.

Learning about this period of time from my godparents' perspective simply deepened my confusion about how to interpret this period of my life. The intensity of these feelings increased when I discovered a letter tucked away in the Memory Box from Pa-ran and Na-nan.

We want you to know our feelings about you and the reasons we want to adopt you into our family. Of course, the number one reason is that we already love you and feel like you are already our daughter. We couldn't imagine our family without you. We were honored and felt proud when we were asked to be your Godparents. We made a commitment to you and God. We meant it with all our hearts. It was easy to love you. You would help mom lead the singing at Sunday School, you would sing with all your heart. Our love grew some more. When we started visiting you at the hospital, you made us happy. It felt good to be with you. We never wanted to bring you back. Our love for you grew some more. Now that you have been living with us our love for you is growing deeper and deeper. We have had good times and bad times and still our love grows. Isn't God good? Brandy you are a very special girl. You have so much to give. We all know there are problems that have to be worked out. We want to be a part of that. We believe we have a lot of love to give you. We want to share the good times with you and when you are hurt, we want to help you get over that too. You've already given us a lot. We want to share your dreams and disappointments. We want to see you grow into the beautiful young lady we know you will be some day. You can be anything you want to be. We know you can do it and we would like to be your parents to help when you need help and to let you do it on your own time when you can. Mostly Brandy we love you. We've got lots of love to give you. We know you've got lots of love to give us. We hope you can hear in this letter some of the reasons we want to adopt you. We love you and want to share our lives with you and have you share your life with us—to be a part of our family!

Even though the feelings expressed in this letter didn't lead to my adoption, my godparents have remained a steadfast presence in my life. We have a bond that has endured the test of time. Though my godfather recently passed, his last whisper echoes in my ear, reminding me of his love: "I love you, my little 'diamond in the rough.'" His endearing nickname reflects his recognition of my potential and resilience. Meanwhile, my godmother consistently highlights a unique quality within me, attributing it to a divine touch—what she calls the "it factor" bestowed upon me by God. Their enduring presence and affirmations have been a constant source of encouragement and gratitude throughout my life.

Despite their willingness to provide explanations long ago, I deliberately chose to leave negative memories behind. Later, in a pivotal moment of my journey, I would find the bravery to confront the unknown and seek understanding. During a visit with my godmother and godsister, I decided to share my revelations and delve deeper into their perspectives.

Delving into the past brought forth heartache and frustration, accompanied by many tears. However, amid the emotional exchange, there was an unwavering affirmation of the type of child I was: "*You were not a bad child,*" my godmother said. "I can not tell you when you did something horribly bad. I just can't tell you." My godmother's perspective, shaped by raising nine children, offered a comforting reassurance that minor infractions and outbursts were part of the childhood experience.

"Regarding the day you left our home," she continued, "the only reason you left is because the psychologist working with you told me, 'Brandy is going to be the kind of person that something will always be somebody else's fault. She's never gonna learn to take responsibility for her own actions.' He suggested that it would be good if you went into a group home where you learned appropriate behaviors and management of those feelings."

I remember thinking, *That's a stupid thing.*

"When Val read the doctor's report, you were abruptly taken from us," my godmother said. "I thought it would be for a short period of time. We had no control, no knowledge of your destination, and naively believed you were coming back. We were left in the dark without any communication with you. Later, we discovered they falsely told you we were getting too old to handle your behavior. That was not true. That was not true.'"

Shocked by these words, I sensed this exchange was intense for all of us. There were harsh truths and raw responses—as we were all taken aback. Yet, in the midst of it all, my godmother reassured me of my strength and potential, emphasizing that I have much to offer the world. Her comforting presence is never failing and affirms me of the blessings I carry—that of understanding. I stopped playing the blame game and questioning the what-ifs.

When I reflect on the conflicting accounts of the day I was moved to a children's home, I feel like the facts probably lie somewhere in between. I'm baffled about how my godparents could be left in the dark without any involvement in the decision-making process, but in the eyes of the law, my godparents were merely foster parents expected to work within the framework established by the state and follow its guidelines. It's not far-fetched to imagine that even a goldfish had more say in my fate than my godparents did!

Instead of dwelling on what happened, I choose to believe that everyone involved had good intentions motivated by a heightened concern and sense of urgency. This understanding lets me focus on the present and cherish the blessing of having my godparents in my life to this day. I recognize that the essence of our relationship is a precious gift, regardless of the circumstances that led to the events of the past.

Reflection

Take a moment to ponder the idea that understanding, like a seed, has the potential to grow and nourish your healing journey. Reflect on aspects of your past experiences or disturbances that you find challenging to understand. Could your reflection shift perspective or provide a sense of clarity? How might embracing and cultivating understanding play a role in your ongoing journey toward healing and self-discovery? Continue to consider what role empathy and compassion play in connecting with others' experiences, especially when dealing with difficult situations. Think about the power of empathetic gestures, no matter how small. How can simple acts of kindness and understanding make a significant difference in someone's struggle?

To deepen understanding, consider these actions:

Practice Active Listening Listen attentively to others without interrupting, allowing them to fully express themselves.

Empathize Put yourself in the other person's shoes to comprehend their feelings, perspectives, and experiences.

Ask Questions Seek clarification and further information to deepen your understanding of someone's viewpoint or situation.

Research and Educate Yourself Take the initiative to learn about different cultures, beliefs, and experiences to broaden your understanding of the world.

Suspend Judgment Avoid making assumptions or rushing to conclusions; instead, approach situations with an open mind and willingness to learn.

Reflect and Self-Assess Continuously reflect on your own biases and preconceptions, striving to expand your awareness and understanding of diverse perspectives.

11

THRESHOLDS OF CARE

Then I went to a therapeutic group home for children.
It was okay except I was the only girl for a while and I was the oldest.

Then I went to the youth home. It was good. I liked it.
But I didn't like the chores & the punishments.

Life Book Entry, February 1987

Case Summary, 1987

Brandy's journey through the adoption process hit a road-
block when her godparents requested its halt, expressing
the desire to have her removed from their home. Following
a recommendation for a small group home, Brandy was temporarily placed in a therapeutic group home for children
until a more permanent solution became available. After
spending two and a half months at the children's home and
just before her 12th birthday, Brandy transferred to an
age-appropriate all-girls youth home.

Initially adapting well in the youth home, Brandy
enrolled in the sixth grade at middle school and maintained
passing grades. She actively participated in recreational
activities and engaged in weekly sessions with her psychologist and group counseling. She also attended a reading
clinic and began learning life skills, particularly cook-
ing. Despite this positive start, Brandy's behavior took a
downturn, exhibiting anger issues, noncompliance with program rules, cursing, temper tantrums, refusal of chores,
and conflicts with staff and residents. Academic struggles arose—inattentiveness in class, acting out in class,
refusal to complete assigned work—resulting in failing
grades and a school suspension.

Meanwhile Brandy met Nancy. Brandy took a liking to her
and their relationship progressed. Brandy's outlook is
promising if the current trajectory of this relationship
is maintained. It is crucial to establish clear guidelines,
set limits, and apply appropriate consequences for her
behavior. Despite Brandy occasionally resisting discipline
and authority, she responds to punishments or restrictions when given. She can be cooperative and delightful,
but creating a structured and guided environment is essential for the success of her placement. As a result, after
fostering a positive connection for five months, Nancy
officially welcomed Brandy into her home on a permanent
basis. Brandy's future involves staying with Nancy until

emancipation. Brandy will need academic support and counseling services throughout her placement. This is essential
to assist Brandy in adjusting and addressing challenges
related to her background as they come up.

✧

Although Val painted a picture of a safe haven for children, as I stepped through the threshold, doubt trickled in. I met the house parent and was taken through the kitchen, past a dining area and a TV/playroom near the stairs. I peeked through an outside window and caught sight of a small play area where children enjoyed the outdoor weather. Upstairs, bedrooms hosted two to three children each. My belongings were neatly placed on one of the beds. This was Val's cue to bid me farewell. She reassured me I would adjust well and promised to check on me soon. In my mind, this sounded all too familiar. Well, at least there was plenty of room to disappear in this maze of a house!

Despite the necessary adjustments for accommodating many children, the overall atmosphere of the children's home was homey, pleasant, and above all, safe. My initial routine involved getting acquainted with the house staff, understanding house rules, and settling into my assigned room. Day-to-day activities followed a set schedule, including wake-up, meals, playtime, study time, chores, bath time, and bedtime, all while attending the neighborhood school during the week, with planned outings on the weekends.

While the environment was generally supportive, there were a couple of children who challenged the house staff with behavioral outbursts, leading to redirection, occasional meltdowns, and timeouts. Remarkably, I don't recall being involved in any reprimands or punishments.

Despite this home not being my ideal place to grow up in, I found myself growing to appreciate it. The structured routine provided a sense of stability, and more importantly, the freedom to be myself and just enjoy being a kid.

Just as I started to feel at ease there, Val dropped the news that I needed to move to an all-girls youth home for a more age-appropriate setting. Reluctantly, I had to accept the change.

The drive to the youth home felt endless, and I had no clue about its location relative to my previous residence. Arriving, I was met with a property that featured what looked like a worn-down, manufactured building. The driveway had passenger vans, so I knew we were in the right place. I was immediately greeted by both house staff and residents. However, my initial dismay was obvious—the residents were noticeably older, and my first impressions were less than favorable.

My instincts kicked in from the initial intake, signaling that this might not be the right fit for me. In a desperate plea, I begged Val not to leave me there, even suggested the idea of going home with her. Despite my reservations, she once again reassured me, promising I could call her anytime, and she would regularly check in. At that moment, I realized my days of being a kid were officially over. I was a lost soul in a place that resembled a house of horrors.

I got to the facility two weeks before Christmas, and it wasn't very Christmassy, with minimal holiday decorations. Honestly, there was no decor to help make the facility feel homey. The main living area was small but there was a big indoor play area and lots of open space outside. Residents navigated a points system, striving to attain higher levels for more privilege. Everything was starkly different from the playful children's home I was accustomed to.

Here the focus shifted to academics, therapy, chores, and occasional outings. The other residents liked me because I was the youngest. But in this new place, I was exposed to unfamiliar behaviors, including foul language, smoking, alcohol, skipping school, and making escape plans to run away. I started not caring much and kind of gave up. I became complacent and indifferent. I figured every few months I'd have to move again and get used to new people and places, so I just went with the flow and didn't get attached.

As I settled into my new surroundings, Val introduced me to Nancy. She was incredibly kind and made a concerted effort to visit me regularly. We embarked on day trips and even had overnight stays at her home. The pinnacle of our time together was an extended visit to Mexico City, Mexico. While vacationing with someone I barely knew seemed unconventional, it turned out to be an incredible experience. Nancy went above and beyond to make sure it was a memorable trip.

⇢ Seeds of Contentment ⇠

There's always more to a story than any one person can remember and learning more about mine from different sources has changed me. When my godparents' placement was disrupted, I couldn't comprehend the reasons, as no drastic events registered in my memory to warrant such removal. However, the children's home was a residential facility catering to children between the ages of 3 and 12, who had been severely traumatized through abuse and neglect. The primary objective of the therapeutic setting was to provide a safety net and equip these children with the skills needed to thrive in a family environment. Now, with a comprehensive view of my troubled past, such a recommendation feels reasonable even if I still find it challenging to reconcile the belief that a children's home could be deemed more beneficial than an intact, committed family.

Reflecting on my time at the children's home, I find no significant concerns. The house staff made a lasting impression, being exceptionally nurturing and attentive. It seemed they developed a fondness for me, likely because I was the oldest child and always eager to lend a hand. My frequent interactions with the toddlers in the playroom might have contributed to this positive dynamic as well. This experience shifted my focus from personal challenges to embracing something positive, casting me into a role as a leader.

One vivid memory stands out—breaking my wrist in a slippery shower incident. Despite the discomfort and frustrations of limited mobility, I unwittingly embodied bravery. It still amuses me to this day, considering it's the only bone I've ever broken.

After a few months, I was transferred to the youth home for girls, and it proved to be less than ideal. As the youngest, I looked up to the other girls as big sisters, but they weren't exactly the best influences or role models. School presented its own set of challenges, mirroring the chaos of the youth home. Feeling out of place, I did my best to keep to myself in an environment marked by frequent fights and a lack of focus on education.

A somewhat traumatic memory from this time was discovering my first period in the school bathroom. In a panic, I sought shelter there until a teacher found me and escorted me to the nurse's office. There, the nurse, keenly aware that no one had prepared me for this, kindly explained menstrual cycles as a natural part of puberty and emphasized the importance of preparation. Too much information, I know. I may be taking the bearing-it-all approaches a bit too far. But in all seriousness, I share this detail because, even now, when doctors ask about the onset of my menstrual cycle, I confidently recall its debut at age 12. It remains my sole concrete medical detail I know with certainty. Yet each time I utter those words, it's like reopening a portal to those not-so-great memories associated with that less-than-pleasant place.

Back then, time didn't matter; I was focused on surviving each day. I remember meeting Nancy when Val introduced us to one another. She was presented as someone wanting to connect and spend time with me, much like a mentor.

We spent a considerable amount of time together, and it was nice, especially the extended vacation to Mexico. Nancy would drop by during the week for dinners or casual visits, and I had overnight passes almost every weekend. I was eager to be in her care, as it was an escape from the pressures and expectations of the youth home. Her home was a more relaxed place where I was not surrounded by stressful events and didn't have to be on guard. I had my own space to chill.

Meanwhile, trouble brewed back at the youth home. I clashed with the other girls who took the nice things Nancy had bought for me, especially after a shopping spree in Mexico at the Guess store. When I returned from weekend passes with Nancy, I saw the girls had used my stuff, and when I stood up for myself, their meanness tormented me. I acted out by disregarding program rules, clashing with staff and peers, throwing tantrums, neglecting chores, and disrupting activities. School wasn't any smoother; I rarely completed homework, disrupted study sessions, and failed all my classes. To make matters worse, I brought my behavior from home to school and ended up suspended.

A few days after a school suspension, I found myself relocating once again, this time with Nancy. Val believed it was in my best interest, considering that staying in the youth home was proving detrimental. I'm confident that both Val and Nancy recognized I was heading down a troubled path—giving up, losing interest in life, and as the youngest in the home, adopting unhealthy coping strategies.

Until now I have been unaware of the timeline that led me to Nancy's home. I find myself questioning—why did she agree to come meet me, take me on vacation four days after meeting me, and sign the foster parent agreement long before I moved in with her? As I piece it together, it hits me that I'll never hear Nancy's side of the story. Instead, I'm left to speculate about the whys, trying to piece together fragments of my story to understand her motives.

I've always suspected Val was keenly aware that Nancy was "my person" and I'm reminded that sometimes the right people come into your life at just the right time, even if someone is behind the scenes helping things along.

Since losing Nancy over a decade ago, I recently turned to Val to help me put the pieces together on how Nancy found me. I discovered that, when the process of my transfer to the youth home began, Val wasted no time in approaching Nancy about taking me in. She expressed genuine concern for my well-being, telling Nancy, "You would be perfect for her. She is savable!" Nancy agreed to meet me but explained to Val that she would have to wait until the beginning of the year because she was leaving for vacation. Upon learning that Nancy was planning to vacation in Mexico alone, Val suggested, "Why don't you take her with you? It would be a great opportunity to get to know her." Without hesitation, Nancy agreed. Val chuckled as she recalled the events, saying, "I requested an emergency court order for Nancy to be your caregiver and requested permission for her to take you to Mexico. I'm sure everyone thought I was crazy, but I just knew this had to happen. I obtained the order, and when the judge signed it, he exclaimed, 'That is one lucky girl!'"

The feeling of contentment these revelations bring me, as I reflect on how they guided me from a troubled time in the youth home to a more stable environment, are immense. While the mystery behind Nancy's decision of "Okay, I'll take her with me!" remains, there's a deep sense of peace in being all right with the unknown. Embracing these moments has helped me recognize the strength that comes with unanswered questions.

In navigating the twists and turns of my life, resolution has required a delicate balance of focusing on the good, digging deep within myself, and acknowledging that some questions may remain unanswered. This approach became a valuable compass to finding peace among life's complexities, helping me find contentment even without all the answers.

Embracing the unknown is an ongoing practice that cultivates a tranquil mental space. Here one can more easily explore past experiences, emotions, and patterns without feeling overwhelmed or driven by negativity. This tranquility forms a strong foundation for healing, promoting clear thinking and emotional stability, which in turn empowers us to confront challenges with clarity and make genuine strides toward healing. It's a journey I've learned to embrace wholeheartedly, finding peace in the fact that some of life's most profound lessons unfold in the spaces between the known and the unknown.

Reflection

Reflecting on this narrative invites you to consider the complexities of sudden life changes and their profound effects. How do swift transitions, unexpected connections, and contrasting environments shape your perceptions and need for reasoning? Have you ever experienced a situation where a swift change significantly altered your life trajectory, and how did you navigate those transitions? In your own life, how have unexpected connections influenced your journey, and what lessons can be drawn from such encounters?

This narrative also prompts contemplation about unresolved questions. How do you personally approach situations where certain answers remain unknown? In navigating life's complexities, do you find comfort in acknowledging that not all questions have clear answers? How can embracing the unknown contribute to personal growth and resilience in your journey? Reflecting on past experiences, how has your relationship with uncertainty evolved over time? Do you believe that accepting the unknown is an essential aspect of maintaining mental and emotional well-being? Can you share a specific scenario where letting go of the need for immediate answers brought a sense of peace or understanding?

To explore contentment, consider these activities:

Gratitude Practice Start a daily gratitude journal where you write down things you're thankful for. Reflecting on the positives in your life can cultivate feelings of contentment.

Mindfulness Meditation Engage in mindfulness meditation to focus on the present moment and develop a sense of inner peace and contentment.

Simplicity Challenge Simplify your life by decluttering your space and reducing unnecessary distractions. Embracing simplicity can lead to greater contentment with what you have.

Nature Connection Spend time in nature, whether it's going for a walk in the park or sitting by a body of water. Connecting with the natural world can evoke feelings of tranquility and contentment.

Acts of Kindness Perform acts of kindness for others without expecting anything in return. Helping others can foster a sense of fulfillment and contentment.

Reflection and Appreciation Take time to reflect on your achievements, experiences, and relationships. Acknowledge your accomplishments and the positive aspects of your life, cultivating a sense of contentment with where you are.

PART THREE

ROOTED RESILIENCE

12

TWEEN TRIALS—NAVIGATING THE CHALLENGES OF MIDDLE SCHOOL

I started visiting with Nancy in December. I left the youth home & went to live with Nancy. I like it. It's cool. I really like not having a lot of chores. School is okay. I plan to stay here until I go to college. I would like to be a school teacher.

The thing I like about Nancy is she is cool.

Life Book Entry, April 1987

Case Summary, 1989

Brandy, a 12-and-a-half-year-old girl, was placed in the care of her foster mother, Nancy, a single, divorced woman in her early 40s. Nancy, a social worker for State Child Welfare has been certified as a foster parent. In recent months, Brandy has grown fond of Nancy, and their relationship has flourished. This has led to the decision to permanently place Brandy in Nancy's home until emancipation.

Brandy is an attractive adolescent who is very demanding and possessive. She is easy to talk with and is very open and honest. Due to past experiences of extreme and ongoing rejection, Brandy struggles with trust, hinting at a potential long-term issue. Building a positive and honest relationship is crucial when working with Brandy, though she remains guarded to avoid the risk of rejection. Establishing trust will be an ongoing process, and careful navigation of her emotional landscape is essential for successful intervention and support.

Brandy initially adapted well to her new environment with continued weekly, individual psychotherapy to address past childhood trauma. Academically, she faced challenges due to attending multiple middle schools in the sixth grade, resulting in gaps in learning, particularly in reading comprehension. Nancy took an active role in seeking an academic setting conducive to Brandy's recovery and success, securing tutoring and enrollment in a reading clinic.

Ten months after Brandy's placement, Nancy agreed to a temporary placement of a nine-year-old foster boy in their home. The initial months seemed promising as they adjusted to their new routine as a family of three. However, signs of resentment and jealousy emerged in Brandy, leading to defiant behaviors, a decline in attitude and effort—especially academically—concerns raised by teachers, and defiant rages.

Brandy continues to battle with distress over disruptions in the home, feeling targeted by her foster brother, and neglect by Nancy, her social worker, and the agency. She perceives deception regarding her foster brother's placement and believes his behavior is negatively impacting her personal well-being and the bond she shares with Nancy. Although Brandy's feelings are consistently validated, she recognizes the extreme stress Nancy is under and acknowledges Nancy is handling the situation the best way she can.

In coping with her foster brother's behavior, Brandy is actively learning survival strategies while awaiting changes for him in the environment. She expresses intense feelings of being cheated and lied to, but begins to accept explanations that, while wrong, the lack of transparency was intended to spare her potential pain. Brandy is now exploring ways to better manage her frustrations and prevent acting-out behaviors. At Brandy's request, Nancy assisted her in acquiring a work permit, enabling her to seek employment. With Nancy's support, Brandy successfully obtained the necessary documentation and secured a summer job. Working at a broadcasting station has proven to be more than just employment for Brandy; it serves as a meaningful preoccupation, offering both a structured use of her time and a valuable means of escape.

Brandy expressed a desire to change her last name back to her given birth name, which Nancy pursued through the legal system successfully. Brandy also expressed a wish to contact her biological mother to address unanswered questions about her natural family. Whether suggested by Nancy or professionals working Brandy, she drafted a letter to her biological mother, which was sent on her behalf. Unfortunately, the response from her biological mother added another layer of emotional complexity to Brandy's delicate situation.

Brandy faced a challenging period marked by suicidal ideations, leading to her hospitalization following a suicide attempt. This critical incident prompted an in-depth assessment during her treatment. It was noted, despite current challenges, that Brandy possesses good and bright intelligence, despite not currently performing at this level, suggesting her capabilities might be hindered by a history of deprivation and abuse. Assessment results from the Stanford Achievement Test indicated that Brandy scored within the average to above-average range, reflecting her intellectual potential. However, there are notable challenges in reading comprehension and math reasoning, where Brandy scored below average. These difficulties are attributed to the frequency of change in both residential and academic settings, reflecting the impact of her unstable environment on academic performance.

Brandy's intellectual capacity is a promising aspect of her overall profile, indicating potential for growth and development. Brandy is actively engaged in ongoing treatment and counseling to address emotional factors that have adversely affected her academic progress. The focus remains on supporting her emotional well-being, acknowledging the interplay between emotional factors and academic performance.

Meanwhile, Nancy worked diligently to transfer Brandy's case to a private foster care agency to better meet her future needs. Through an extensive referral and intake process, Brandy met the criteria for services and was accepted into the program. The case was successfully transferred, marking a pivotal step in addressing Brandy's ongoing challenges and fostering a more supportive environment for her development.

Approaching the end of eighth grade, Brandy faced the need for a new school as her current one concluded at this level. Nancy, placing importance on a Christian and quality education, applied to various reputable private schools. Despite facing multiple rejections, she secured admission to a smaller private school.

Despite academic accomplishments, lingering issues surrounding her mother intensified. As eighth-grade graduation celebrations unfolded, Brandy combated thoughts about her mother's absence while in the presence of everyone else's parents. This emotional turmoil manifested in threatening temper tantrums and feelings that she could not regain control and would possibly hurt herself or someone else. This prompted Brandy's reentry into an inpatient treatment hospital for adolescents for severe depression. The treatment program involved a comprehensive approach, incorporating group, individual, and family therapy to address past abuse, depression, and possibly obsessive-compulsive behaviors. Brandy is navigating some really heavy struggles at such an impressionable and critical age.

Responding to Brandy's request upon exiting the treatment program, Nancy arranged a face-to-face meeting with her biological mother to address unresolved issues, though this was ill-advised. The encounter echoed the sentiments expressed in an earlier letter, with her mother wanting nothing to do with her, leaving Brandy disappointed. However, she found some relief in having some lingering questions addressed through her mother's dismissal. This confrontation marked a pivotal moment in addressing the emotional complexities behind Brandy's challenges, particularly her difficulty in releasing the desire for reconciliation and forgiving her mother for the neglect and abuse she experienced.

=≺⊹ ⊹≻=

At this point in my journey, fate led me to an exceptional woman named Nancy, who had witnessed my acting out and stubborn behaviors. Despite this, she extended an invitation into her home. Entering Nancy's oasis, I carried with me a self-erected wall, a survival mechanism I had adopted to shield myself. Hesitant to let anyone in, I found comfort in building barriers rather than bridges, echoing the fight-or-flight response ingrained within me.

To be brutally honest, I wasn't exactly making life a walk in the park for myself or anyone. I questioned whether I truly deserved a stable family. At this juncture, I carried the assumption that every year or so, life would uproot me, hurling me into a new environment, forcing me to adapt to new rules and overhaul everything about myself.

In this whirlwind of uncertainty, Nancy stepped in, making my initial adjustment to her home surprisingly smooth and providing a comforting atmosphere. Nancy, a single woman—professional, strong-willed, and a devout Christian—went from living a peaceful lifestyle into parenting a broken and lost 12-year-old. Stepping into the role of a parent not bound by blood, during the tumultuous years of adolescence, is unquestionably a courageous undertaking.

Despite developing a liking for Nancy, I approached her home with uncertainty and apprehension. Initially, nights were plagued by intense nightmares, imprinting memories of the past on each waking day and deepening my confusion. I established a pre-sleep ritual that involved meticulously looking behind window drapes, into closet doors, and beneath the bed, driven by unsettling paranoia.

Observing my repetitive actions, Nancy delicately inquired about my routine, prompting me to admit my quest to ensure no one was hiding. Instead of criticizing, she compassionately reassured me each night, accompanying me on bedtime rounds to confirm there were no lurking threats and no one coming for me. This ritual persisted until her comforting presence dissolved my anxieties, allowing me to gradually abandon the need for nightly security checks.

The initial months unfolded smoothly as we settled into a new routine: school, church, therapy, health care appointments, and check-ins with Val. A significant highlight was reconnecting with my godparents, facilitated by Nancy's outreach to them, transforming us into an extended, blended family. Nancy and my godparents even seemed to navigate a co-parenting dynamic seamlessly. This extended family collaboration became evident when Nancy and my godparents joined forces to address concerns about my schooling. Nancy's worry about my continued attendance at the neighborhood public school prompted coordinated efforts to secure admission to the school affiliated with my godparents' church. This small Christian school ultimately proved to be an ideal fit for the remainder of my middle school journey. The familiarity the teachers and staff had with me from my time with my godparents ensured a smooth transition and seamless acceptance into this educational environment. Despite these positive developments, the path through middle school wasn't entirely without challenges.

As I settled into my new home, Val brought forth a situation to Nancy, one that would impact me too. Sensing the significance, Nancy involved me in the conversation and consideration.

"There is a young boy, nine-years-old, in need of a placement for two weeks," Val explained.

Nancy hesitated, mindful of the adjustments our household had just undergone, given its small size and the recent establishment of our routine.

"Sure, we will take him," I volunteered.

Nancy, still hesitant, questioned the logistics. "Are you sure? Where will he sleep?"

I reassured her. "We'll make it work—for only two weeks."

Consequently, this young boy entered our home temporarily, marking a shift in the trajectory of what had initially seemed to be a comfortable and secure environment.

What was initially meant to be a brief two-week placement evolved into a commitment that extended over months. The transition from a temporary arrangement to a long-term commitment challenged my sense of security, as the circumstances surrounding his prolonged stay remained unclear. Unaware of why his previous guardians hadn't returned for him, I battled with feelings of insecurity.

Nancy eventually shed light on the situation, explaining that there was no available home for him. She expressed a personal dilemma, stating that she couldn't consciously ask him to leave. Despite my understanding, given my own past as a child in need of a home, I couldn't help but feel resistant and bitter. We engaged in further discussions, eventually reaching a consensus that opening our home to him on a long-term basis was the right thing to do. As the honeymoon phase in my new home came to an end and a foster brother entered the picture, the shift in attention did not sit well with me.

I perceived the addition of a foster brother as a threat to my security and the undivided attention I had grown accustomed to from Nancy. My foster brother was a handful, requiring considerable TLC. Both of us, coming from traumatic experiences, lacked appropriate coping strategies. Despite attempts to get along, our relationship was marked by extreme ups and downs. I saw us as two entirely different people with seemingly nothing in common, except for our shared experience of foster care. My strong-willed, self-centered, bossy, and resentful demeanor only fueled the challenges. I harbored deep resentment, as my world was once again turned upside down. From my perspective, the original plan was simple—just Nancy and me, without the added complexity of another person in the mix. The once calm and easygoing atmosphere transformed into chaos and dysfunction, creating a home of feast or famine. Juggling our care during this turbulence, Nancy faced numerous challenges. I, however, did not make it easy for her, spiraling down a rabbit hole and resorting to self-sabotage with an "I don't care" attitude. I was convinced that this newfound turmoil was bound to bring an end to any sustained goodness in my life.

Well into seventh grade, I successfully adjusted to my new school environment and continued therapy to address unresolved feelings from the past while learning effective coping strategies. One significant realization was my deep-seated resentment toward carrying the family name from the adoption. The name reminded me of the disgust I held toward my adoptive parents. In response, Nancy graciously facilitated a legal name change, allowing me to reclaim my given birth name.

Engaged in therapy, I tried to confront and resolve the deep-seated anger stemming from my past, particularly the difficult reality of my mother giving me up. The subsequent months were a blur while I wrestled with overwhelming emotions. I descended into depression, ultimately reaching a critical point that led to a suicide attempt. Following this, I found myself in the emergency room, undergoing assessment and receiving treatment for spiraling out-of-control behaviors.

Meanwhile, Nancy worked diligently to transfer my foster care case to a private agency, recognizing the potential for long-term benefits and better preparation for my independence. Val and Nancy's persistence in the application process proved successful, and my case went under the care of this agency. This transition meant once again navigating a new program, forging relationships with different case managers, and adhering to new program policies, expectations, and goals. Val was no longer my advocate or contact in times of trouble. I guess even advocates needed a break from my life's chaos!

⇥ Seeds of Acceptance ⇤

Looking back on my past, I recognize that if I had had the wisdom I now possess, my adolescent years could have been profoundly different—marked by increased connections, stability, and fulfillment. Accepting this and looking back, it's apparent that Nancy is the champion of my story. To convey the essence of this extraordinary woman, let me share an excerpt from a testimony she provided, a touching discovery tucked away in the Memory Box.

When God Calls Your Name: This marks my tenth year as a foster parent. What started out as a seemingly flip remark "I'll take her" in a conference room full of fellow social workers has turned out to be an awesome walk with God. Reflecting back, I realize the many changes that have occurred in me and in the children who shaped my life. They have taken me places I would have never gone, offered experiences I would have never had, encountered systems I would have never known, some of which I hope to never know again. In all this my faith has been strengthened. God truly works in wondrous ways. He calls us into this ministry called foster care and sustains us and the children in many ways. I find it is not always possible to do things the convenient, familiar, conventional and hassle free way if I want to grow and help others grow. When God calls your name, he will provide a way!

As I reflect on this perspective, I accept that the depth of my own selfishness was profound, acknowledging that I once believed I was the sole recipient worthy of Nancy's affection. Initially, seamlessly slipping into her home fueled my desire for an exclusive connection with her. However, the arrival of my foster brother diverted her attention and focus toward meeting his needs, or so I thought. In hindsight, I was masking and deflecting my insecurities by blaming my foster brother. While his presence in the home may have triggered some unresolved feelings from my past, my own problems would have surfaced with or without his presence. Contemplating the what-ifs of whether my life's trajectory would have been different with or without him is a complex puzzle, cloaked in uncertainty. Yet, amidst this uncertainty, one thing remains clear: Nancy's unwavering commitment and sacrifices. She gave everything selflessly, ensuring both my foster brother and I were not just surviving but thriving. In light of her dedication, there's no room for a blame game. After all, even I cannot bear the burden of denying someone their place in the world.

It was also during this time I found myself harboring resentment toward Val. It seemed she had a knack for popping up at the most inconvenient times, stirring the pot of my already complicated life. Now, after chatting with Val, I get it—her intentions when placing my foster brother in our home weren't to ruffle my feathers, and it's clear Nancy's heart always had room for both of us. Who could argue with that? Well, probably just the stubborn teen in the house, clamoring for extra attention and pushing for curfews that stretch into next week!

While I accept that there was a lot of trial and error in my healing process, the plan of reconnecting with my mother at this time is still a confusing sore spot. I don't recall if writing a letter expressing my innermost feelings to her was suggested by a therapist or someone closely working with me, but up to this point, I had no knowledge of my mother's whereabouts or any means of contact. Someone thought it was a good idea to initiate this on my behalf.

Within the Memory Box, I found a copy of the letter I had written, paper-clipped to the original response from my mother, complete with the addressed envelope. The revelation was jarring, and reading the five-page response remains an emotionally crushing experience.

Unfortunately, legal constraints prevent me from sharing the letter word for word, but it took on a cautionary tone that accused me of deceitful behavior—lying and stealing—asserting there was no need for witnesses, as the truth was supposedly self-evident. It claimed my half sister wanted nothing to do with me because I tried to put her daddy in jail. It was a desperate plea for innocence on behalf of that same man, insisting he would never harm any child in inappropriate ways. My mother's haunting conclusion questioned how I could inflict all this on her, accusing me of not loving her and declaring there was no hope.

One friend who I dared show the letter to expressed disbelief at a mother's words about her child, saying, "This is sickening. How could a mother ever speak about a four-, five-, and six-year-old child in this manner? Everyone knows the only reason a child steals food is because they are hungry." Another friend was unable to continue reading due to heartbreak and disgust. Yet another empathetically questioned, "Did you read this as a child? What kind of person writes this to a 12-year-old? How did you survive this?"

In response to their reactions, I couldn't help but joke, "Well, my mother was obviously mentally unstable. Doesn't everyone have a dysfunctional family member? It's practically a rite of passage! If I don't laugh, I may end up crying, once again!" It was the only rational explanation I could offer.

The rock-bottom part of my journey up to this point, four months after receiving the letter, was the suicide attempt. Though the specifics leading to the event evade my memory, I vividly recall a profound sense of being lost, hopeless, and confused as I approached the end of middle school. I didn't genuinely want to die, but I yearned for the overwhelming feelings to dissipate and for my mind to find peace. My desire was to start anew, break free from the turmoil of the past. I desperately wanted to leave everything behind, and to shed the label of being a foster kid. Working with therapists, I was encouraged to focus on delving into my past and acquiring effective coping strategies for dealing with the pain. They led me to believe the only pathway forward was to confront and relive my experiences by opening up to someone. However, talking about my past repeatedly made me feel hurt all over again, and I couldn't see a better way to stop this cycle.

Clearly, I did not handle this letter well and I internalized every word. Even though I can't completely recall the letter, having likely blocked it out, there is a distinct memory of feeling a sense of madness during that period. I was convinced that everything was a product of my imagination—that I had fabricated it all, and consequently, it was entirely my fault. As my thoughts manifested, I descended into a profound ache, one from which I felt powerless to escape. This despair infiltrated my daily functioning, prompting me to seek comfort any way I could, or in my case, to contemplate putting myself out of misery.

Reflecting on Nancy's unconventional approach after the attempt to end my life—encouraging a face-to-face meeting with my mother—brings a unique perspective. Perhaps traditional therapy methods proved insufficient for my healing. I remember Nancy disapproving of programs and therapists that readily labeled my diagnosis and prognosis, focusing only on the challenges without providing hope for the future. It seemed that Nancy trusted that a "see for yourself" or "see it to believe it" approach would offer me closure and allow me to distance myself from the past to move forward. Now I understand that Nancy leaned toward a more holistic approach, treating me as a whole person rather than solely addressing specific symptoms or issues. There were so many times I would say to Nancy, "You sure don't act like a social worker. Aren't you supposed to know better? You do things so differently. It's like you're on a secret mission to redefine the job!" But in the end, she knew exactly how to handle me.

If only all the mental health professionals I encountered had offered a glimpse of a more positive future—a vision of overcoming challenges and planning for success—maybe I would have accepted the things I could not change sooner. I wish they had guided me with the perspective that "this too shall pass," encouraging me to look beyond my current problems and focus on a brighter tomorrow. Instead, I spent years feeling like I was on a hamster wheel, endlessly running in place with no way out. The pain remained, and hope was never offered. The healing methods I encountered were, in my view, impractical and ineffective. Disheartened, I withdrew further, burying the pain deeper, hoping it would one day fade into oblivion.

In lieu of talking about my feelings and internalizing my mother's hurtful words, which fostered a belief in self-blame and unworthiness, I wish someone had helped me visualize proving her wrong. She hinted in the letter that she took pleasure in others' failures with me, using it to validate her actions. So why not turn the tables and prove that she was the one with issues all along? I needed support to counter her manipulation, to shake off the feeling of being driven to madness, and forge ahead with resilience, accomplishment, and acceptance of who I was. I could have benefited from encouragement to pursue my passions and from guidance in setting tangible goals to build my confidence. Someday I might have the opportunity to throw it all back at my mother, demonstrating what I've achieved despite her undeniable volatility.

I am grateful for the wisdom I have gained over my adult life, learning about alternative ways to heal, like practicing self-compassion and mindfulness to stay grounded and surrounding myself with supportive friends who uplift me. Additionally, techniques like cognitive behavioral therapy (CBT) to reframe negative thoughts, journaling to process my emotions, and participating in community activities to create connections have all been invaluable. It's not a one-size-fits-all process, and finding what works for me has made all the difference in accepting my life as it is and appreciating myself for me.

Practicing "Seeds of Acceptance" means starting to understand and be okay with something—a situation, one's self, or a challenging reality. It's taking the initial steps toward finding comfort in yourself. It's a gradual process of growth, where understanding and acknowledgment play crucial roles in cultivating a more positive and constructive perspective over time, similar to how a dandelion seed slowly flourishes into something strong and resilient.

Reflection

My journey, marked by confrontations with painful truths, emphasizes the impact of internalizing others' words and how this shaped my perception and actions. How do external influences shape your self-perception and acceptance? Are there specific aspects of yourself or your experiences that you find challenging to accept? Engaging in the blame game or what-if scenarios is often unproductive. What are the underlying reasons for the tendency to do this? How does this behavior impact your emotional well-being and ability to move forward? What lessons can you extract from past experiences without getting caught up in assigning blame and instead shifting your mindset toward problem-solving and growth? Reflecting on alternative approaches to healing can open up new paths toward well-being. What traditional healing modalities have you explored and what have been their effects? Are there alternative healing practices that transcend conventional therapy methods that you are open to exploring? Moreover, how do you strike a balance between accepting responsibility for your actions and recognizing when you aren't ready to face certain truths? In what ways can acceptance contribute to a more positive and constructive outlook on your life and experiences?

To promote acceptance, consider these activities:

Acceptance Letter Write a letter to yourself acknowledging and accepting your strengths, weaknesses, and past mistakes. Embrace yourself with compassion and understanding.

Mindfulness Practice Engage in mindfulness meditation or activities that encourage present-moment awareness. Practice accepting your thoughts, emotions, and sensations without judgment.

Self-Compassion Exercise Practice self-compassion by treating yourself with kindness and understanding, especially during challenging times. Use affirming statements to affirm your worth and value.

Letting Go Ritual Create a symbolic ritual to represent letting go of past grievances or disappointments. This could involve writing down what you want to release and then burning or burying the paper.

Gratitude Practice Cultivate acceptance by focusing on what you're grateful for in your life. Keep a gratitude journal or simply take a few moments each day to reflect on the positives.

13

TEENAGE TURMOIL—SURVIVING THE HIGH SCHOOL YEARS

*Nancy, you have been the only parent to me. I know I am hard to deal with.
I want to try and make myself happy. I have never been able to say I feel good
about myself as a person. I want to try and not be dependent on you as much.
I am persistent and stubborn, but I think we are both alike in those areas.
Deep in my heart I know I love you. All I want is for you to understand.
I want to change and I really want to be the perfect daughter but there is no such
thing. I want to be the best I can and I want you to help me. If I make the wrong
decision on something I will learn from my mistakes. I want you to accept that.
You are a parent but you will not be there all my life. I need you so much
in my life now more than ever.*

Life Book Entry, June 1990

Case Summary, 1994

An appealing adolescent, Brandy, exhibits a strong, possessive nature, though she remains communicative and
forthright. Progress across various treatment aspects
is evident, but she still needs ongoing individual therapy, group counseling, and educational support. While
required to take part in agency activities—particularly a
skills-building group, social skills group, and independent living group—was mandated, Brandy's non-participation
was influenced by her resistance to accept the agency's
foster care plan and Nancy's lack of support of recom-
mendations and interactions. Observing Brandy's desire
for control, Nancy recognizes and accommodates this need.
Nancy frequently questions the necessity of disrupting the
status quo and is reluctant to involve Brandy in agency
groups, believing it's unnecessary for her to be consistently associated with other foster youth. She expressed
disagreement with the agency's involvement in her family
matters and mentioned that she would take on the responsibility of adopting Brandy if the agency decided not to
provide services due to conflicting viewpoints. While it
might seem like Nancy undermines agency support, her primary commitment is to Brandy. Nancy prioritizes Brandy's
needs, ensuring her overall well-being remains paramount.

Brandy's demeanor has become more subdued, showing reduced
demand and control. Ongoing concerns involve academics,
social drinking, risky behaviors, and legal incidents.
Brandy usually owns up to her actions, and she felt especially upset about needing to repeat the ninth grade because
she didn't have enough credits to move up. She understands
it's a result of her own choices. Efforts to establish a
structured home environment and resist Brandy's demands
are underway, with the social worker guiding Nancy to not
give into Brandy's negotiation skills. Brandy once again
was evaluated and was found to be extremely depressed,
with suicidal ideations, hopelessness, worthlessness, and

irritability, diagnosing her with major depression, recur-
rent type. She was prescribed Prozac and is working on her
past abuse, depression, social skills deficits, family
difficulties, and trust issues.

As Brandy matures, she appears to operate at an ele-
vated and more positive level. However, emotionally, there
are aspects of her life that she seems to have pushed deep
into her consciousness. A notable concern is her tendency
to initiate but not follow through with treatment in various areas of her life, especially with the prescribed
Prozac and various forms of therapy. Brandy's therapist
suggested a specialized treatment with his associate to
address issues from her past. Hypnosis was to help Brandy
recall events that might still trouble her. However, after
a few sessions, Brandy felt uncomfortable and decided to
stop the treatment. These instances highlight situations
where, with Nancy's help, she has been allowed to discon-
tinue therapy.

Brandy is putting in diligent effort at school, consistently achieving grades that range from average to above
average. Her commitment is evident, as she has been recognized with merit awards in Math and English, along with
an athletic award for her achievements in tennis. Brandy
works part-time, and it seems to bring her joy. She demonstrates competence and a commendable work ethic. She has
expressed interest in college and was encouraged to consider the agency's continuing education and job training
program. It is an application process and if accepted, the
program is a contractual agreement where participation
is mandatory in an independent living group. In return,
Brandy may qualify for self-sufficiency assistance and
scholarship for furthering her education.

Nancy expressed immense pride in Brandy's well-rounded
education and perspective, having been entrusted with
delivering the benediction at the high school baccalau-
reate. Nancy observes that Brandy is socially adept and
well-suited to achieve her goals. While her academic

achievements might not be the highest, she compensates with dedicated effort. Nancy appreciates Brandy's responsible approach to planning, effective time management, and reliable execution of responsibilities. Brandy also demonstrates self-awareness by recognizing when she needs help and appropriately seeks assistance.

Brandy earned a spot in the agency's career, job, and education training, securing a scholarship for further education. Her acceptance into her preferred college marks a significant achievement, and she plans to reside in the dorm while undergoing progress monitoring. Skillfully preparing for the transition from home to dorm life, Brandy independently arranged all the necessary details for independent living.

Despite moving from home, she maintains a connection with Nancy, going home on Sundays for church, lunch, and laundry. This demonstrates Brandy's ability to balance newfound independence with ongoing ties to her support system.

Nancy is optimistic that Brandy's life is aligning to enhance both her physical and emotional well-being. She attributes this positive transformation to Brandy's deepening relationship with God and her sense of stewardship, foreseeing ultimate healing and prosperity. Even though this marks Nancy's final update, she remains committed to supporting and reinforcing Brandy, ready to advocate for her whenever necessary.

⇌┼⇋

Involved with mental health therapy, academic remediation, and agency and social work intervention, my schedule became inundated with appointments under the watchful eyes of various professionals. This limited my freedom to experience a semblance of normalcy. The array of interventions aimed to address different aspects of my well-being created a structured but somewhat restrictive routine as I completed my time in the system.

My days were dominated by therapy—a carousel of therapists and varied approaches that, in my perception, yielded little benefit. I found it challenging to let down my guard and establish a genuine connection. My attitude reflected a resistance, skeptical of outsiders claiming to comprehend my experiences. I often questioned how they could understand when even I struggled to make sense of it all.

During my high school years I was grappling with a series of challenges that unfolded gradually. Academic pressures, social issues, strained peer relationships, and the burden of mental health stressors collectively shaped a difficult and demanding experience. While there were undoubtedly positive moments, the weight of my failures unfortunately overshadowed them, making it challenging for me to recognize or appreciate those accomplishments.

Navigating a new chapter in a small private high school, I found myself labeled as the "new kid" in a community where most had grown up together across K-12. Carrying the weight of recent challenges, I felt isolated, convinced that my unique background was incomprehensible to those surrounded by intact and well-off families. The stark contrast in backgrounds, coupled with my personal struggles, modest family lifestyle, and foster care status, created a sense of separation because my life was so different. Trying to fit in made high school feel even more complicated.

I stuck with what I knew, hanging out with friends I'd already known. Also, I gravitated to the "cool kids," even though some saw them as troublemakers. Nancy wasn't thrilled with my choice of friends. She wanted me to find stable and positive influences, hoping I'd leave behind the troublesome connections and be influenced by the church-going teens. Most of the people I surrounded myself with came from broken homes, faced challenges in school, and had issues with rules and authority. While being around them allowed me to be myself without pretense, it eventually became clear that they didn't really like me for who I was.

A few things stood out about my freshman year. Our home had only a few house rules, like keeping the bedroom tidy, completing weekly school work, adhering to curfew, and attending Sunday school and church weekly. The firm "no Friday and Saturday night activities" consequence of not complying was nonnegotiable, but I often found ways to manipulate or avoid it.

My foster brother served as a helpful distraction, drawing Nancy's attention away from my escapades, but whenever I needed Nancy, she was consistently there. Particularly, she was supportive when two of my friends died by suicide within weeks of each other. She attended the services with me and helped me navigate through the grieving process.

Following these tragedies, I went on a school retreat where I met an upper-classman, and upon our return from the trip, we became fast and close friends. I began drinking alcohol and became preoccupied with my social life; I looked forward to the weekends hanging out with the much older crowd. I mastered being home by curfew and then sneaking out my bedroom window for late-night parties.

My first serious trouble happened a couple of weeks before my fifteenth birthday, when I had my initial encounter with law enforcement. With the permission of a friend, I, along with others, made an unauthorized entry into her house while her parents were away, resulting in a rowdy party and property damages. I endured a severe hangover and a stern reprimand from the sheriff's office for my role in the unauthorized party. Four of us were charged with illegal entry and criminal damage to property. In juvenile court, one of the other parents was able to negotiate a settlement for all of us, and the criminal charges were dropped. This should have taught me a lesson, but after being grounded for weeks, I spiraled into more significant issues. I continued drinking, neglected school, and placed excessive focus on my social life and dating, often engaging in reckless activities. Failing the ninth grade didn't come as a surprise to me, but Nancy was disappointed, as she had secured multiple tutors to help me. She established some rules that I was to complete certain tasks over the summer before regaining any sort of social life. I managed the bare minimum to get my privileges back.

A painful incident on July fourth, marked by heavy drinking and a harsh fall, left me bruised and injured. Yet, I continued my drinking habits and faced another blow. At an out-of-town concert Nancy had taken myself and some friends to, I succumbed to heavy intoxication. Nancy, discovering my state, insisted on an immediate return home. In a resistant act as we headed home, I opened the van's sliding door and jumped out of the moving car. The ambulance came and I went to the emergency room. My blood alcohol level was 2.82 and I sustained a jacked-up jaw, scratches and bruises, much like road rash.

Waking up in my bedroom with a throbbing hangover and my body aching, the aftermath of that night unfolded. Nancy entered the room, her demeanor calm yet concerned, saying, "Last night your life was spared. God wants you here, and so do I. I imagine you can't remember much with your dangerously high alcohol level, but in the emergency room while they were pumping your stomach they mentioned it was a sort of blessing that you jumped out of the moving car. If you had fallen asleep on the two-and-a-half-hour ride home, you might have slipped into a coma and never woken up. Mull over that as you recover in the next few days."

Throughout the years, Nancy and I had cultivated a unique form of communication that we fondly termed "love letters." These were more than just notes; they became a way for us to express our thoughts in the moment. The process involved writing down our feelings, allowing each other the time to absorb the words on paper. After my blunder, she left a letter on my dresser saying, "When you are ready to confront whatever is going on with you and figure out where to go from here, I am here for you." Days later we discussed how I was going to address this incident with the agency and therapists. Further, we discussed my peer group and the influence they had on me. To round out our conversation, Nancy established some restrictions and rules to ensure my safety.

Disclosing the incident to all the professionals involved in my life added to my stress and gave them more control. Another mental health evaluation followed, focusing on depression and substance abuse. The recommendation was Prozac for depression and intensive weekly therapy. Initially, the medication seemed promising, but after a few months, I underwent a transformation— low energy, subdued mood, and a pervasive disconnection from everything and everyone. The constant numbness and isolation became intolerable, leading me to halt the medication in a bid to reclaim my outgoing personality. Nancy supported this decision, as it granted me some much-needed control over my well-being.

Reluctantly, I found myself back in the same school, repeating the ninth grade. At this point, I was two years older than my classmates, and my so-called older friends seemed to have abandoned me. They not only distanced themselves but actively encouraged others to do the same. I faced a barrage of negativity, rumors, and acts of meanness, becoming the unfortunate target for the "mean girls."

To navigate through this challenging phase, I kept busy with work outside of school. Additionally, I rekindled friendships beyond the school environment and returned to church youth group activities. Doing things outside of school helped me escape from the problems and challenges I was dealing with in school.

I successfully navigated my second attempt at ninth grade, but I certainly didn't do it alone. A particular godsend entered my life in the form of a science teacher. While I was sitting alone in the school library, he walked up, introduced himself, and struck up a casual conversation. His kindness was evident as he offered me an open invitation to stop by his classroom anytime for assistance with anything. A retired military professional turned educator, he affectionately referred to me as "Kid," a nickname that resonated with me. This remarkable individual became not just my school tutor but also a cherished ally.

Throughout the remaining three years of high school, things got better. I still had all the eyes on me, lots of therapy sessions, and extra help with school. On top of that, I had to comply with the agency, attending social and independent life skills groups, which I wasn't too excited about. There were good times and some tough moments, but I kept going. Gradually, life started feeling more normal. I was working part-time jobs, active in school and church activities, mission and volunteer work, and even making connections with fellow classmates. During these years, I would feel like I was making progress, but then things would go backward, especially in a couple of situations involving alcohol. I had a not-so-memorable incident when I accidentally swallowed a toothbrush, and to boot there was another incident with the law.

The toothbrush incident was a desperate attempt to avoid facing the consequences of my alcohol indulgence from the night before, or perhaps to escape the day's responsibilities. After a heated argument with Nancy, I vaguely remember rushing to the bathroom. Out of anger, I began fiercely brushing my teeth and suddenly started vomiting. The relief from vomiting led me to continue jabbing the toothbrush in my mouth and down the toothbrush went. Realizing I swallowed it, I rushed to Nancy for assistance. Nancy initially doubted my claim, but X-rays confirmed the truth. Surgery was necessary to remove the object. I bear a lifelong scar as a reminder of this impulsive and excruciating experience.

The other incident happened at 18 when I found myself facing a driving under the influence (DUI) charge. Pulled over on my way home, I admitted to drinking, and a breathalyzer registered a 19 percent alcohol concentration. The officer took me to the station to wait for Nancy. In an attempt to spare her disappointment and potential stress, I pleaded with the officer not to contact her and to lock me up instead. I was willing to endure a stint in a cell, convinced that Nancy would have had enough and the agency would react sternly, possibly leading to expulsion from their program.

Contrary to my expectations, I was released to Nancy, and life continued with a DUI first offense charge, community service, MADD classes, and probation. Finally, with this experience, I reached a turning point and moved toward a more focused and responsible path for a while.

Two weeks before my 19th birthday, my friend and I embarked on an unannounced trip to see my biological mother. Despite not having her address, familiarity with landmarks guided us to her place of work, which I remembered being near my former home. During the two-hour journey, we strategized on what to say—I had reached a point in my life where I felt courageous enough to confront her. I aimed to let her know that, despite all the hardships, I was doing fine without her. In case I lost my nerve to confront her, I drafted a letter as a backup, which is still buried deep in the Memory Box, explaining that my whole life I had held onto my love for her and couldn't fathom how she could cut me out of her heart so easily. Specifically, if she knew she didn't love or want me, why didn't she give me up at birth rather than allow me to develop a bond only to rip it away? My goal was to have the last word, close the door for good, and head off to college without the baggage.

Upon arriving, we noted the business name and phone number on the office door. However, I immediately felt overwhelmed and considered turning back home. Instead of entering the office, I returned to the car. My friend insisted that we had come this far and needed to see it through, so she jotted down the phone number. We then drove a mile down the street and parked at a hotel. We decided to give my mother the chance to meet us. While my friend used the pay phone to call the number, I retreated to the bathroom, not wanting to witness the unfolding events, and waited for her to update me.

My friend informed me that my mother answered the phone and requested that we stay put, saying she could meet us at the hotel in 15 minutes. Shocked and panicked, we rehearsed what I was going to say. When my mother arrived, I stood still, ready to deliver a rehearsed speech or hand off the letter about self-love and closure. However, before I could begin, she surprised me by running to me for a big embrace, expressing happiness that I had come back.

Despite my prepared sentiments for closure, I ended up at her kitchen table, talking about life. I learned I had a half brother in addition to my half sister, and the same stepfather who, from a distance, supported my mother's newfound desire for me to be a part of their family. Throughout this, my mother consistently vocalized her strong desire to have me in her life. She shared baby pictures of me and photo proofs from her wedding with my biological father, creating a surreal moment.

I excelled in my senior year of high school, was on the verge of graduation, got accepted to my preferred college, and received an education grant from the agency for complying with their independent living initiative. Alongside this, I continued to build connections with my biological mom and her family. Navigating these new ties was confusing, as trust was a challenge, especially around my stepfather. But surprisingly, all four of them—my biological mother, stepfather, half sister, and half brother—attended my high school graduation, celebrating the day with me. Nancy encouraged reconnection, understanding that I felt something was missing and believed that rediscovering my roots might fill those empty spaces. However, she also cautioned me, emphasizing the importance of my voice. She advised me to steer clear of situations that could potentially cause me harm once again.

During my freshman year of college, my life felt complete. Reuniting with my mother and half sister was a dream come true, and being in college was an accomplishment I hadn't imagined reaching. Then one day the realization hit me that this rekindled connection was not in my best interest.

I was experiencing real highs and lows, and heavy drinking and partying became a significant part of my life again, leading to my ultimate failure in college. I'm certain that the internal struggle regarding my reconnection to the past, the unanswered questions, and allowing it all back into my life, was my downfall.

It all came to a head at a family cookout where my boyfriend and I were present. During the party, a moment occurred that woke me up, and I mean it was like a splash of cold water to the face. My stepfather approached me when I was alone, and I immediately tensed up, feeling like the scared six-year-old child I once was. He expressed happiness about my reunion with my mother, urging us to let go of the past. In that vulnerable moment, my mother walked in, sharing her joy at having the whole family back together again. Then, in a consoling manner—well, about as sincere as she could get—she dropped a bombshell, attempting to rewrite my memories. She claimed that a relative who temporarily lived with us was the one who had sexually abused me, not my step-father. According to her, the state had been threatening them, and releasing me from their home was the best option for my well-being. Overwhelmed, with tears streaming down my face, I couldn't grasp what was happening. In a frantic state, I exclaimed that I couldn't do this. I grabbed my boyfriend, packed my things, and left, never looking back. That was the moment I reclaimed my life and forged my own path, truly free from the past.

⚜ Seeds of Affirmation ⚜

It's fair to say that, while with Nancy, I was a handful and bucked the system often. I acted out, engaging in irresponsible and foolish behavior. I was headstrong, determined to navigate life independently. Amidst the challenges, a few factors stand out that led to growth and set me on a positive path forward.

First, there was Nancy. As an adult, I am profoundly reminded of Nancy's selfless acts and unwavering persistence to keep me on track. One incident, in particular, stands out where she displayed remarkable fearlessness. During a heated argument, I impulsively grabbed the car keys, stormed out of the house, and jumped into the car with the intention of fleeing the situation, perhaps never returning. Nancy, undeterred, ran after me and attempted to get into the car, but I had locked the doors. She proceeded to lay across the driveway to prevent me from backing out. I screamed for her to move and let me go. In response, she defiantly shouted, "Over my dead body will you run from this." Pleading for her to release me, I revved up the engine, threatening to back out as I inched toward her body. She never budged and yelled, "You have a choice, and I pray to God you choose wisely." Moments later, I pulled the car forward, put it in park, and turned off the engine. At that moment, I genuinely believed Nancy was crazier than I was, which provided some comfort. I mean, who sanely puts themself in harm's way? After a few moments, I got out of the car, walked behind the vehicle, and found her sobbing. Gently, she said, "When you are ready to talk, I will be waiting." I entered the house and retreated to my bedroom. Over the next few hours, I contemplated the gravity of what had just occurred and realized if this wasn't love, then I didn't know what love was. She was willing to sacrifice her life to ensure I did not do something reckless. Many years later, I asked Nancy how she survived all I put her through. Her response: "By the power of prayer and prayer warriors. God had a plan for you and I was the vehicle God was using to get you there."

Next, I can't discount therapy, even though it didn't work that great for me. It left little room for exploring my own aspirations. I believe it would have been more advantageous to meet me where I was, guiding me toward my unique path of growth, inspiring me to look beyond my struggles. In essence, challenging me to discover who I was beyond my circumstances.

Nancy was always prepared to adopt me in the event it became necessary. Surprisingly, I was unaware of this fact until we broached the subject during my wedding planning. Nancy, being perceptive, understood my emotions tied to adoption, considering my previous experience with a failed adoption. To clarify, it was in my best interest for Nancy not to adopt me. Adoption would have meant losing the financial support and means that provided me with numerous advantages, including private school, academic tutoring and remediation, health care, college assistance, and support for independent living—all of which I received through the private foster care agency.

As I approached graduation and aging out of foster care, the agency directed its attention to life after foster care through its independent living program. Although I was resistant and slow to start with the program, it proved to be an invigorating experience. It granted me the opportunity to envision a future for myself and it was most definitely instrumental in my success. I consider myself fortunate to have had both the agency support and a foster mother who didn't show me the door when the foster care subsidy ended, leaving me on my own without any preparation.

Another bright moment throughout my adolescent years was writing, particularly poems. When faced with challenges at school or home, I would retreat, put pen to paper, and unleash my thoughts on the blank lines before me. Revisiting these writings tucked away in the Memory Box offered glimpses into my adolescent struggles and the perseverance required to overcome them.

The Memory Box also keeps my silent angels close—those who have touched my life. Whether it's a handwritten note or a faded photograph, each speaks volumes of the kindness and support I received during my darkest times. Even my high school science teacher left a memento that ended up in the box. Our connection endured well into my adulthood, and going through the Memory Box I stumbled upon a letter addressed to Nancy from him. I believe she meticulously placed it there for me, anticipating its discovery.

March 2006

Dear Nancy,

Sorry I did not get to see (our kid) Brandy when she came through. I have enclosed a note that was in her Biology book that she turned in at the end of the semester. I don't know if she wanted me to have it or not. I kept it anyhow. It really shows the hurt/ pain that she went through, so young in her life.

She said that she was writing a book (do not know what it is about) and the enclosed note may be of use for her. I am very proud of her and how far she has climbed. Use judgment as to passing it on to her.

Brandy owes you so much as many kids don't make it, even with better conditions. Thank the Lord you were there to take her in and guide her in the proper direction and thought. You are both Mother and angel to her as she realizes that now. I never fussed with Brandy, because she would make me laugh, just being a wonderful kid!

Also enclosed are several pictures I found while going through some of my old school notes, etc.

Poem of Life!
by Brandy

If I was on a mountain top, I would jump
If I would stay in school, I would probably flunk
I try to love and try to care
I try to be my own person but
I seem to always find myself in a curse
I always wonder how my life would be if I was alone
I would probably see how life would be for my own
I would love to see real family
And sometimes maybe real friends
If I am lucky I will not die
But God or someone would have to strike with their stride
I listen and get scolded
I try to understand but then people just say hold it
I feel my life is on hold or strike
Running from one sin to another
I really wonder if I will get out of this hole
I wish there was an answer that someone could tell
But I probably still end up in hell
People may think I am doing things for pity
But their wrong, I'm frustrated and not that strong

I can only hold so much pain otherwise I would go insane
If I didn't love or care, I couldn't imagine I would have gotten anywhere
My heart gets broken over and over
I wish my life was innocent as a four leaf clover
I was born as an innocent child with my whole future ahead of me
I've gone place to place, home to home, heart to heart
I've gone into circles and now I'm torn apart.

I was left speechless the first time I saw this in my Memory Box and I thought back to the quiet gestures of encouragement and unwavering support of my science teacher, along with the power my poetry had to help me through. Belief in me, like my science teacher had, made a profound impact on my journey, and looking back, it's amazing to know they were right. I could do it.

The Memory Box holds one last artifact that strikes me as profoundly significant, though it's for other reasons. It's the original copy of the second letter from my biological mother, written to me in the spring of my senior year in high school. This letter takes a different tone, expressing love for me. In essence, this letter unfolds a narrative of a mother grateful to have her complete family again, finding it increasingly challenging to be apart from me—stating that this is my home. She professes immense pride in the wonderful person I've become, expressing a wish to take credit for it but acknowledging her gratitude for Nancy. Her only hope is that Nancy will continue to share me, suggesting the possibility of me having two moms because Nancy deserves the right to remain my mom. The letter concludes with an affirmation of her love, expressing the desire to be my mom again, and praying she never loses me. Also, tucked behind the letter was the only birthday card I have ever received from my mother, wishing me a happy 20th birthday. It reiterates her love for me, hoping that soon our love will overcome all our misfortunes of the past. Expressing how proud she is of me and to say that she is my mother.

Having the complete picture of our entire relationship behind me now, I feel affirmed in my ultimate choice to let her go. I wonder why I was so insistent on having a relationship with her. Despite the pain she caused, I had still yearned for her love and acceptance. Looking at it academically, it became evident that my longing for a connection with my biological parents, even in the face of hurt, probably stemmed from a profound need for love, acceptance, and identity. The bond a child forms from birth, known as the primary attachment bond, is crucial. It is established with the primary caregiver, typically the mother or father, and lays the foundation for the child's sense of security and trust, significantly influencing their social and emotional development. Even when taken away, there remains an inherent longing for understanding and reconciliation, driven by a deep-seated desire for belonging and closure. This foundation of biology, psychology, and emotional attachment underscores the complexity of these emotions. Realizing this, I found relief, understanding that I wasn't alone in experiencing these sentiments. It confirmed that I wasn't intentionally sabotaging my life; rather, I was navigating the enduring effects of a bond formed at birth that couldn't be erased.

Fortunately, Nancy's reassuring voice resonated in my mind as I struggled with my relationship with my biological family, gently affirming the importance of self-love, acknowledging my inherent worth, and empowering me to use my voice. Nancy's guided wisdom served as a light when I needed it most, enabling me to assert control and discover my inner strength.

The biggest affirmation I received to date did come from my mother who, through her roundabout way of talking about the past, inadvertently validated my memories of abuse. While she did try to deflect them away from my stepfather and place them on someone else, admitting they'd happened at all affirmed I wasn't crazy and I didn't create the trauma in my mind. With these realizations to empower me, I made the decision to walk away from my biological mother and never looked back. I vowed to myself that I would never allow my past experiences to shape me into anything resembling her. That day, I affirmed my strength and resilience. I honored my ability to recognize the truth, embrace my validation, and move forward with confidence.

Reflection

Affirmations are positive statements or thoughts that support personal growth and healing. They serve as a foundation for cultivating a positive mindset, fostering self-love, and promoting resilience during healing. As you reflect on the themes of your life through the challenges and triumphs of the human spirit, what or who contributed to your enduring capacity for healing? How can these experiences affirm your ability to navigate difficulties and emerge stronger? How can external validations from others serve as affirmations of your worth, capabilities, and competence? Lastly, how can these experiences serve as affirmations of your capacity to contribute positively to the lives of those around you? Challenge yourself to recognize and celebrate the richness of your experiences, viewing them as a collective tapestry of affirmations that reinforce your strength, resilience, and the unique qualities that shape your journey.

To delve into affirmations, try these activities:

Practice Positive Self-Talk Replace negative thoughts with positive affirmations, reminding yourself of your strengths, capabilities, and worth.

Keep an Affirmation Journal Start a journal dedicated to writing daily affirmations. Include positive statements about yourself, your goals, and your worth.

Surround Yourself with Positivity Spend time with supportive people who uplift and encourage you, reinforcing positive affirmations.

Write Gratitude Letters Write letters to yourself expressing gratitude for your qualities, achievements, and resilience. Read these letters whenever you need a confidence boost.

Keep a Vision Board Create a vision board filled with images, quotes, and affirmations that represent your dreams and aspirations. Display it somewhere you'll see it every day.

Make Affirmation Cards Make a set of affirmation cards with positive statements written on them. Carry them with you and pull one out whenever you need a reminder of your worth.

Practice Self-Compassion Be gentle and understanding with yourself, acknowledging your efforts and growth, even in moments of setbacks or challenges.

14

CHOICES THAT DEFINE US

Life presents us with a myriad of challenges and setbacks, each with the potential to shape our journey in significant ways. However, it is not the mistakes we endure that define us, but rather the choices we make in response to these adversities. The decisions to learn, grow, and persevere through hardships reveal our true character and resilience. It is through these conscious choices that we forge our identity, demonstrating our ability to adapt and thrive despite life's inevitable difficulties. Ultimately, it is these defining choices that carve out our path and shape who we become.

I refused to be defined by my mistakes or seen as a failure. I wanted my life to mean something and, quite frankly, to be the opposite of my biological mother. I fought hard to get my life back on track, driven by confidence and a need to align my head and heart. Eager to find my purpose, I carefully considered my options and committed to the most tangible steps available: faith and education. Although faith is considered intangible, rooted in belief rather than physical evidence, I found that its effects manifested tangibly in actions, emotions, and experiences. When it came to education, it truly was my ticket out. I dedicated myself to my studies, transferring to a smaller college where I excelled, and then returned to the university with renewed focus and determination.

Balancing the demands of independent living and returning to the church brought me comfort. Actively participating in church and young adult activities became central to my routine, and I assumed a role in the church youth group. The church community has always embraced me, offering a welcoming refuge as I navigated the journey of self-discovery. Nancy's deep connection to the church was a constant guiding force, and her steadfast involvement helped create a safe space filled with acceptance and understanding that I could return to when needed. Within this faith community, I found liberation from past struggles and a renewed sense of optimism, reminding me that I am not alone on this path.

At 23, it might have seemed unconventional, but I wholeheartedly embraced my spiritual journey. I began praying daily, seeking guidance and clarity. Each day, I asked God to help me surround myself with well-intentioned individuals, to guide me in understanding my true self, and to possibly lead me to someone with whom I could share my life. Even though my prayers felt somewhat selfish, I sincerely sought God's guidance and prayed for Him to reveal His plan for my life.

After I spent a year practicing intentional living, Brian entered my life. We met at church, and sparked a friendship that swiftly turned into a serious relationship. I was pretty sure it was all part of God's plan. Brian had his life together—college graduate, professional, ambitious, and stable—typically not my type. His experiences were vastly different from mine; he came from an intact family and had embarked on many worldly experiences. Despite our dissimilar backgrounds and interests, I found myself captivated by his intelligence, stability, and fearlessness. What stood out the most was the freedom we granted each other to be ourselves. We didn't have to be glued at the hip for our relationship to flow effortlessly. The constraints of our other commitments limited our time together, but the ease with which our connection unfolded made every moment meaningful.

On a nice fall day during football season, we headed out for a weekend getaway to Brian's college alma mater for a big game. We were excited about the weekend plans, and I was eager to meet his college friends and enjoy some tailgating fun. Little did I know, beyond the excitement of the game, this weekend held an even more significant moment. Brian surprised me with a marriage proposal, expressing his desire to spend his life with me. Stunned, and without hesitation, I happily responded with a resounding "Yes." Jackpot!

As we kicked off wedding plans, it was a whirlwind. I was graduating from college that spring, and Brian had job opportunities in another state. We picked a spot for our new life as a married couple, and he moved there months before the wedding. We set the wedding date after my graduation, so I stayed back to finish school, maintaining a long-distance relationship until I could join him.

Things were moving fast—Brian and I traveled back and forth to sort out wedding details, buy our first home, plan the move, and even attend a marriage encounter retreat. In the midst of all the busyness, Nancy adopted me, allowing Brian and me to successfully navigate the marriage license application process.

Shortly after the adoption, an unexpected realization hit me. I would soon be leaving Nancy and relocating many hours away—essentially, leaving behind the person who had given her all for my survival. I struggled with the idea of inadvertently subjecting her to the same abandonment I had always feared.

Expressing my concerns to her, I admitted leaving didn't feel right. She responded with understanding, acknowledging that it would be difficult, but she emphasized the importance of doing challenging things. Nancy encouraged me to put distance between myself and the place that housed many unfortunate memories, to start fresh without the influences of the past. She assured me that we would be fine despite the miles between us.

On a breathtaking day, my beloved godfather walked his "diamond in the rough" down the aisle of the church where Brian and I first met. Surrounded by a couple of hundred family and friends, Brian and I exchanged our vows. The effort and generosity of everyone involved made our wedding day truly unforgettable. Each person went above and beyond to create a magical experience, sparing no expense to turn my dream wedding into reality. From the intricate floral arrangements to the elegant venue, every detail was carefully crafted to perfection. And, yes, even a horse and carriage made an appearance, adding a touch of whimsy and leaving us feeling like royalty.

⊱ Seeds of Sacrifice ⊰

I once heard that "God sets the lonely in families," and as I reflect on my journey, I come to understand the profound truth in those words. Nancy was a divine blessing, the perfect mother chosen for me. My in-laws have also been an incredible gift, embracing me wholeheartedly and becoming my greatest supporters. Beyond my godparents and extended godfamily, my newfound cousin clan, faith community, and circle of friends have been steadfast champions, offering unwavering support and comfort along life's winding paths.

In the Memory Box was a note from Nancy. It read:

This meditation on scripture contains a reflection on your wedding by a church member. I received a copy and thought you might appreciate having it:

If the Holy Spirit is the continuation of the presence of Jesus, we must remember that Jesus celebrated the joyous occasions of life many times. Last Saturday, many of us witnessed a beautiful wedding in the sanctuary. On Sunday, I mentioned to Chris what a lovely ceremony he had performed, and he said he had a difficult time holding back tears. I confessed that everyone in our row was teary-eyed. It wasn't because we were sad; it was because most of us knew the difficult beginnings of this beautiful young lady's life. Now, she was experiencing a storybook ending, living happily ever after. Early in life, she had been adopted in Christ, and just before her wedding, she had been legally adopted by a loving, spiritual person of this church. The Holy Spirit was at work here, and we were witnesses to His goodness through the actions of others.

As I reflect on this, it resonates with a deep sense of connection and reminds me of the village that brought me to where I am today.

As Brian and I approach our 24th anniversary, I find myself deeply grateful for the truly blessed life that we have shared together. Let me be clear: blessed, not always easy! Brian continues his career with the same company that marked the beginning of our married life, while I furthered my education, earning a master's degree in counseling, and now work as a professional school counselor. Our two children have recently entered adulthood, spreading their wings, turning their hopes and dreams into reality.

Meanwhile, Brian and I are starting to navigate the empty nest phase, investing time in getting to know each other again. We are rediscovering shared interests, planning new adventures, and savoring the quiet moments together. This journey of reconnecting has brought a fresh sense of excitement and intimacy to our relationship, proving that even after 24 years, there's always more to discover about each other.

Leaving everything behind to build the life I dreamed of was more than necessary—it was crucial. Nancy, as a loving parent, not only validated my needs but encouraged my chosen path. She often reminded me that I was finally in control and my wants and needs mattered. This gave me the freedom to pivot into the future, finding my way on my terms. Although Nancy often described my approach as "stubborn," she never withheld her support. She sacrificed so much so that I could experience the life I have today fully. If this isn't the embodiment of a divine parent, mother, and grandmother, I don't know what is.

Years after high school and college were a distant memory, I asked Nancy why she thought I was stubborn, as I had always perceived it as a negative trait. She confessed, "Your stubbornness was what made you a survivor. Your strong-willed personality did not allow you to give up; it was a force to be reckoned with." Amen to that!

"Seeds of Sacrifice" can promote healing on your journey by symbolizing the intentional and nurturing acts of selflessness and support we take to build a rewarding life. When someone like Nancy plants seeds of sacrifice, it represents the care, love, and dedication invested in your well-being. These acts serve as a basis for growth and healing, fostering a sense of security and resilience. They served as a foundation to help me begin my married life in a new place, where I could control the narrative. When you recognize sacrifices, it creates an environment that helps you grow and emotionally recover on your life's journey.

Reflection

Reflect on instances where leaving past experiences behind was an intentional act of kindness to yourself. How did distancing yourself from certain situations contribute to your well-being and overall sense of peace? Consider the sacrifices you made by letting go of past experiences. Were there moments when you prioritized your mental and emotional health over clinging to situations that no longer served you? Identify supportive individuals who may have played a role in encouraging you to move forward from past experiences. How did their kindness and support contribute to your ability to forge a better life?

Explore the idea of self-compassion in the process of leaving behind past experiences. How can you acknowledge the courage and strength it took to make those decisions, viewing them as seeds of sacrifice for your own growth? Think about the intentional acts of kindness you can continue to practice for yourself as you navigate forging a good life. What steps can you take today to nurture your well-being and build a positive path forward? Remember that leaving behind past experiences is a continuous journey. Reflect on the progress you've made and consider how ongoing intentional acts of kindness and support can contribute to the continued forging of a fulfilling and positive life.

To explore the concept of sacrifice, consider these actions:

Personal Reflection Take time to reflect on moments in your life where you've made sacrifices, whether big or small. Consider the motivations behind these sacrifices and the outcomes they led to.

Interview Loved Ones Interview family members or close friends about sacrifices they've made in their lives. Listen to their stories and reflect on the impact of their sacrifices on themselves and others.

Clarify Your Value Understand what matters most to you and be willing to prioritize those values, even if it requires personal sacrifice.

Focus on Long-Term Goals Keep sight of the bigger picture and the potential benefits that may come from making sacrifices in the present.

Find Meaning Seek meaning and purpose in the sacrifices you make, recognizing that they contribute to personal growth, relationships, or larger causes.

CONCLUSION: FINDING PEACE IN ENDINGS

As we conclude this emotionally charged and rewarding healing journey, I invite you to ponder one final reflection. Recently, during an exercise with a soon-to-be high school graduate, the question "What is your why?" emerged—a question I had never been asked before. My purpose, or "My Why," crystallized as I realized that, for me, God is not flawed in His plan and He is the driving force. It compels me to inspire others to walk their walk—to liberate themselves from the shackles of past pain, embrace the challenges, appreciate the experiences, and reassure them that they are not alone on the journey.

In paying tribute to the life of my unsung hero, Nancy, I share the profound "Why" that echoed through her testimony delivered eight years before her passing. This enduring conviction is a precious treasure that will forever be etched in my heart.

Ticket to Ride: I was asked yesterday to be a substitute for today's speaker. I immediately thought, How appropriate in that much of my life work has been the work of a substitute—a substitute parent. Some fifteen years ago I became a foster parent of children who were born to other people and had come into the foster care system. I raised these children to adulthood and now profoundly call them my own.

I never thought of my personal entry into the world of foster care as a "ticket to ride" but I have considered aspects of it as a call from God and given much thought and prayer to how answering that call to be a foster parent has shaped my faith journey over the years and how it has been a journey of healing, not just for my kids but for myself. Suddenly, I was living the work that was my chosen profession. I was a professional Social Worker who had worked in the field of Child Welfare in Child Protection, Foster Care and Adoption my whole career. I had "talked the talk". Now I had to "walk the walk".

The urge to become a foster or adoptive parent had crossed my mind several times but I had dismissed it as impossible. If I did not think I could have handled children when I was married, how could I manage being a single parent to other people's children with no family support system or friends willing to back me up in this undertaking? Also, I worked full time and thought I did not have the time or the means for children. But when God invites you to do something for Him, He provides the means. And in my case, it was the church. People are always commending me on how well my children have turned out. I am reluctant to accept the credit, knowing that I was simply God's agent. It was God's people in this church who were Christ to me and my children who made the difference. As they say in the African American tradition, "It takes a village to raise a child".

I will say that I am a stronger person and better Christian for having joined in the loss and suffering of my children. The pain of rejection is great and it is so tempting to follow the world's ways of dealing with the pain rather than to let Christ be the healer. God was my lifeline and I was determined I was not going to let Satan have my children.

A former pastor of this church said something I will never forget at a critical time in my life of parenting. He said that many parents are reluctant to influence their children in matters of faith, thinking they should let them make their own decisions. But if you don't influence them, you can bet someone else will. Right then I determined to use my authority to influence them for Christ.

When I became a foster parent, I was of the opinion that I did not have a lot of fixed opinions or house rules. But it did not take long to realize what my values were in comparison to those that were brought into my home. As a foster parent you receive much advice and counsel from helping persons and professionals on behalf of the children. Foster care is a shared parenting experience by nature. In all this through the years, coupled with my faith journey, I have come to realize a simple truth—that values are imparted through relationships, not rules. Rules are to promote healthy relationships. I came to have only three rules that were nonnegotiable.

1. *My children had to attend church and Sunday School weekly until they graduated from high school, after which they could decide for themselves;*
2. *My children and I sat down to meals together without the TV on and no one could start eating until everyone was served and we asked the blessing; and*
3. *If my children had an issue with me that they wanted to resolve, they had to talk to me directly about it rather than go through a counselor or someone else although I encouraged them to use a counselor to help them shape their understanding of the situation.*

Without going into details, these simple rules have provided order for our lives that otherwise were in chaos. These rules have brought us into relationships with many friends and adult mentors in the church which lead to a closer relationship with God in Christian community and shaped our faith in Christ as the Savior and Master Healer.

In closing, I would like to share a scripture that I have used daily to prepare me for wilderness experiences and deliverance during my foster parenting ride. Isaiah 40:31. It reads, "They who wait upon the Lord shall renew their strength; they shall mount up with wings as Eagles." I have come accustomed to waiting on the Lord over the years. I am waiting now for direction from God now that my foster parenting responsibilities are essentially over and my children are choosing a life in Christ for themselves. I thank God for the people in this church daily who were and are Christ to them and to me. In closing, I would like to say that for me Lent is a time for allowing God to remove some of those things in our lives that are separating us from God and His endless possibilities for our lives.

As we part ways, I invite you to reflect on a quote by Carl Jung, the founder of analytical psychology: "I am not what happened to me, I am what I choose to become." While interpretations may vary, for me this quote underscores the idea that, although we cannot erase our past, we can transform our experiences into wisdom. By shifting our perspective, we can commit ourselves to self-improvement and forge a path to success.

Stepping boldly into the future, unburdened by the weight of the past, I embrace a newfound clarity about the experiences that have shaped me. I fully accept that my healing and growth have spanned decades, driven by a mission to break free from the cycle I was born into and carve my own path. This recognition of my purpose resonates deeply within me, compelling me to mold my life into something meaningful. Like a dandelion dispersing its seeds in the wind, I aim to spread the essence of my journey far and wide, creating a legacy of resilience and transformation.

This journey is not a sprint; it's a marathon. It demands a significant investment of time, patience, and persistence to nurture those seeds into fruition. It's about allowing them to take root and blossom into something extraordinary.

For me, telling this story was in alignment with God's vision for my life, offering me my purpose. In the end, this precious gift was not about the destination but the journey itself, offering me an appreciation of who I am and the blessings I carry—my life and my healing!

As you journey forward from this memoir, may God's blessings accompany you now and forever, empowering you to flourish and thrive in all your endeavors, and may you always choose to become the best version of yourself.

ACKNOWLEDGMENTS

To my husband. You have been my steadfast supporter and unwavering believer. Thank you for your constant encouragement and for propelling this endeavor into motion. Your faith in me means everything.

To my family. Thank you for your steadfast love throughout this journey, for loving me unconditionally, and for always seeing the good in me. Your support has been my foundation.

To my circle of friends. Your inspiration has been the catalyst for this journey and the sharing of my healing. Oh, how I wish I had a quarter for every time you asked, "When are you going to write that book?" Your persistent encouragement has been invaluable.

To my writing mentors and professionals—Wendy Cocke, Lesly Gregory, Rosemarie Perry, Cathy Fyock, and PAGES. Thank you for bringing this memoir to life with your positive and invaluable expertise. Your guidance has been instrumental in this journey.

To my Heavenly Father. It is through Your perfect timing and grace that this endeavor has come to fruition. Thank You for guiding me every step of the way.

ABOUT THE AUTHOR

Brandy McCachren is a seasoned professional school counselor with 20 years of dedicated experience working with children, adolescents, and young adults. Having grown up in the foster care system, Brandy brings a unique and deeply personal perspective to her work. She is passionate about helping young people develop essential life and coping skills, paving the way for their independence and success.

Brandy actively advocates for programs that can help individuals discover who they are and who they want to become. Drawing from her own life experiences, she connects with the individuals she works with by empowering them to look beyond their current circumstances and focus on what they can control. Her commitment to this work is driven by a genuine desire to make a difference in the lives of those who, like her, have faced significant challenges. Through her advocacy and mentorship, Brandy continues to inspire and guide young people toward brighter futures.

Brandy can be reached at: www.resilienceroadadvising.com

REVIEW INQUIRY

Hey, it's Brandy here.

I hope you've enjoyed the book, finding it both insightful and inspiring. I have a favor to ask you.

Would you consider giving it a rating wherever you bought the book? Online book stores are more likely to promote a book when they feel good about its content, and reader reviews are a great barometer for a book's quality.

So please go to the website of wherever you bought the book, search for my name and the book title, and leave a review. If able, perhaps consider adding a picture of you holding the book. That increases the likelihood your review will be accepted!

Many thanks in advance,

Brandy McCachren

WILL YOU SHARE THE LOVE?

Get this book for a friend, associate, or family member!

If you have found this book valuable and know others who would find it useful, consider buying them a copy as a gift. Special bulk discounts are available if you would like your whole team or organization to benefit from reading this. Just contact resilienceroadadvising@gmail.com or visit www.resilienceroadadvising.com.

WOULD YOU LIKE BRANDY MCCACHREN TO SPEAK TO YOUR ORGANIZATION?

Book Brandy Now!

Brandy McCachren accepts a limited number of speaking/coaching/training engagements each year. To learn how you can bring her message to your organization, email resilienceroadadvising@gmail.com or visit www.resilienceroadadvising.com.

www.ingramcontent.com/pod-product-compliance
Lightning Source LLC
Chambersburg PA
CBHW082011140626
46553CB00021B/2782